EARLY GEORGIA WILLS AND SETTLEMENTS OF ESTATES

WILKES COUNTY

By

SARAH QUINN SMITH

CLEARFIELD

Reprinted for
Clearfield Company, Inc. by
Genealogical Publishing Co., Inc.
Baltimore, Maryland
1992, 1996, 1998, 2003

Originally published: Washington, Georgia, 1959
Reprinted: Genealogical Publishing Co., Inc.
Baltimore, 1976, 1983
Library of Congress Catalogue Card Number 76-025331
International Standard Book Number 0-8063-0735-8
Made in the United States of America

FOREWORD

Wilkes County, created in 1777, is the parent county of all of Elbert, Oglethorpe, and Lincoln, part of Warren, Greene, and Taliaferro, and part of Madison and Hart, cut from Elbert (originally Wilkes).

The records in this volume are supplemental to Mrs. Grace Gillam Davidson's two-volume work, Early Records of Georgia: Wilkes County (1932, 1933), and are designed to assist interested persons in making a quick survey of most of the oldest records in the Ordinary's office, once known as the Inferior Court office. In the Superior Court office the old books are voluminous and begin with complete records of the first court in Wilkes County, held in 1779 in that part of Wilkes later known as Lincoln County.

The first U. S. Census (1790) was lost by fire. Statistics from that census gave to Wilkes County approximately one-third of the population of Georgia, census returns having been made just prior to the date Elbert County was cut from Wilkes.

Wilkes County owes a debt of gratitude to Secretary of State Ben Fortson, Jr., and to Mrs. Mary G. Bryan, Director of Georgia Archives and History, for the restoration and microfilming of the Wilkes County records, and to the Clerk of the Superior Court and the Judge of the Court of Ordinary for their cooperation in this work.

The compiler wishes to express appreciation to Miss Ophelia A. Gilmore of Austin, Texas, for making the complete index, to Mrs. Lucile Pierson of Holly Hill, Florida, for encouragement and for typing these records, and to Mr. William Johnson of Washington, Georgia, for mimeographing this book.

Sarah Quinn Smith
1959

CONTENTS

Wills, Originals, 1787-1815 1

Original Documents, loose papers, Partitions of Estates, Equity Court Cases, Chancery Court Records 6

Divisions, Real Estate Inheritances, Deeds of Gift, Deed Books, Superior Court 13

Settlements of Estates by Administrators and Executors 21

Wills, Book 11 (200 wills altogether) 35

Some Original Marriage Bonds 60

Index 63

WILKES COUNTY

ORIGINAL WILLS

Wills are filed by family name in the Office of Judge of Inferior Court. Date of drawing is first, followed by date of probating.

- - - - - -

ALEXANDER McALPIN, of Wilkes Co. July 10, 1784; Sept. 28, 1790. To wife Mary McAlpin, who lives on the place, one third of my movable estate. To my stepdau. Ann Hagard, and stepson, Jonathan Hagard, gifts. To my eldest son, Robert McAlpin, my bounty land warrant, 575 acres, except the money I received from him which is six crowns, three dollars and four guineas. To son, Solomon McAlpin 200 acres on the old Tugolo path. To son, Alexander, lands. To my three little sons, 200 acres on Savannah River at Cherokee Ford and 200 acres in South Fork of Broad River, the lower part of that which I gave to Alexander McAlpin, I desire to be divided among Samuel Major Temple McAlpin, William Alexander McAlpin, and William David McAlpin. To my four daus. Jenet McAlpin, Elizabeth Barberry McAlpin, Mary, and Sarah Temple McAlpin. My six youngest children to be schooled in English and Arithmetic. Exrs. Alexander McAlpin and James Little. Wit. John Sigman, Mary Saxon, Agnes Moore.

JOHN WILKINSON, Esq., of Wilkes Co. Apr. 9, 1785; Aug. 26, 1786. To wife Ann Douglass Wilkinson valuable property other than her right of dower. To dau. Sarah Harwood Jones the pair of diamond earrings and diamond ring that belonged to her grandmother Hulda Wilkinson. To daus. Ann and Caroline Wilkinson a diamond ring each and cash. To eldest son Micajah cash, four negroes, when 21 years of age. To sons Reuben and John cash and four negroes, each, when 21 years of age. To Aunt Joanna Wilkinson, of Smithfield, Rhode Island, annuity of 70 pounds for life. All other property to be divided and delivered to all my children by my wife as she sees meet. Exrs: Wife, Ann Douglass, Abraham Jones. Wit: Hazelwood Wilkinson, Thomas Grant, Abraham Jones.

Note: Copy of the Will of John Wilkinson was loaned to the compiler by Mrs. Robert S. Towers, 1854 Montgomery Place, Jacksonville, Florida. Probate date recorded in the back of Will Book 1810-1816 in old script.

ELIZABETH BRUCE of Wilkes Co., Ga. gives to her beloved daughter, Sally Ross Edmunds (widow) fifty acres of land on the waters of Kittle Creek adj. Moores land and Flurrys land and the land of John Jarrell: that at my death the land is to belong to my daughter Sally R. Edmunds, to dispose of as she pleases. May 28, 1834. No Exr. Wit: Geo. M. Johnson. Proved Sept. 7, 1835.

PHILIP THOMAS. June 3, 1786. Five shillings to each of my beloved sons and daughters: John Thomas, Mary Newton, Augustain Thomas, Rachael Cooper, Ann Jones, Elizabeth Holmes. Mentions his land on Clouds Creek to be sold; proceeds to be divided between my two daus. Margaret and Hannah Thomas. To son Benjamine lands, one half tract, after my youngest son comes of age. To son Edward the plantation I live on, furniture, negroes, etc. To wife Mary household furniture, horses and mules for use on her plantation during her life, then to Edward. A special negro, Sil, to wife, then to Edward. Exrs: Wife and son Benjamine. Wit: Thomas Brown, Ann Brown.

THOMAS HAMPTON of Wilkes Co. Dec. 18, 1788; Dec. 1, 1791. To son Benjamin Hampton my plantation. To dau. Margaret Metcalf land. To son Thomas Hampton. All other estate to son Benjamin, who is Exr. Wit: Philip P. Highnote, Julian Nail, William Hampton.

WALTER M. GIBSON. Oct. 15, 1787; Nov. 20, 1791. To wife Judah for life. To son Sylvanus Gibson after death of my wife. Gifts to dau. Mary Hogan, 200 acres of land where I now live. To dau. Piety Davis (not Patsy Davis as in the published record). Exrs: Son, Sylvanus, son-in-law, Griffin Hogan. Wit: Stephen, Thomas and Wm. Johnson.

MILES DUNCAN of Wilkes Co. Aug. 13, 1789; Apr. 18, 1791. To wife Ann my land on Kettle Creek, adj. John Cargile, Jno. Edwards, and David Duncan, and notes on James Ware of "Ogeechee Co." Ga. and all estate for her support and that of my children. Exrs: John Ogletree, Ann Ogletree. Wit: David Duncan, Isaiah Philips, Sarah Duncan.

ISRAEL BURNLEY of Wilkes Co. Nov. 19, 1789; Jan. 7, 1791. To son Israel Burnley. To dau. Susannah Barksdale. To dau. Frances Smith. To dau. Elizabeth Burnley. To son Stephen Burnley the land on which I live, after death of my wife. To dau. Ann. Terrell Burnley. To gr. son Henry Brown. All other estate to wife. Exrs: Wife Hannah, sons Henry and Stephen Burnley. Wit: Benj. Thompson, Richard Fretwell, Benj. Sizemore.

JOHN HEARD, SR. of Wilkes Co. Feb. 2, 1787; Mch. 20, 1788. To my well beloved granddau. Jane Austin, my negro girl Julia, also all furniture of every kind. To granddau. Sarah Germany, "who is the eldest dau. of Bridget Staton, and to her youngest dau. Bridget Staton", all the rest of my property, but that my wife shall keep the whole estate in her hands to rear and educate my gr. dau. Jane Austin, until the decease of Bridget H eard, my wife. I appoint my son Stephen Heard, my son-in-law Joseph Staton, my nephew Jesse Heard exrs. Wit: Jesse Heard, William Hardeman.

Remark: Exrs. bond of date Mch. 20, 1788, Joseph Staton, security. The Will is recorded in Will Book C, pg. 36.

BENJAMINE NICHOLSON. Mch. 18, 1790. To my wife Judah. To dau. Polly Nicholson. To Apsilla Horn, at death of my wife, the plantation I live on, reserving to Keziah Davis the small piece of land where she now lives. Exrs: Adam Jones, Arthur Fort. Wit: Sarah Linicum, Arthur Fort.

OWEN GRIFFIN of Wilkes Co. Aug. 5, 1789; Apr. 3, 1790. To wife Ann all estate during widowhood for her use and for my children. Exrs: Josiah and Benjamine Stovall, my brothers-in-law. Wit: Ephraim Pharr, Richard Griffin.

Ephraim Pharr

JOHN BOWEN. Oct. 4, 1790; Oct. 16, 1790. I leave to wife all that her father gave her, negroes, horses, furniture. To sons Horatio C. Bowen, Esq. and ? Bowen, all other estate. Exrs: George Matthews, John Matthews, his son. Wit: (illegible). Proved on the oath of John Matthews.

JOHN COLBERTSON. Aug. 8, 1789; Feb. 2, 1790. Wife, Polly all estate for life. To my youngest dau. Nancy at death of my wife, a negro Philis and furniture, etc., the said dowry to be clear of expense of her education. To my children that are unmarried, cash, at their marriage. Residue to children Thomas and John Colbertson, Mary Goss, Nichodemus C. Philpot, Martha Colbertson and Fanny Colbertson Philpot, each to have three years schooling. Exrs: Martha and son, John Colbertson. Wit: John Colbertson, Christ. Hargreaves, Reuben Allen.

1790

WILLIAM JACKSON of Wilkes Co. Dec. 2, 1790; Mch. 12, 1791. To wife Ellender Jackson my plantation, furniture, negroes, horses, etc.; all to be divided equally among my children at death of wife. Mentions son John Jackson. Exrs: Wife, son William, Thomas and Henry (or Jerry?) Jackson. Wit: E. Price, Thomas Nelms.

E. Price Thomas Nelms

MICHAEL WHATLEY of Wilkes Co. Feb. 16, 1788. To my youngest son Elisha, 200 acres where I now live, and mahogany furniture. To dau. Franky Mason, deed of gift. To sons, Thomas and Jesse. To dau. Caty Morgan. To grandson Hiram Whatley, son of Richard Whatley, and Frances, his wife. To son John. To sons Michael and Daniel. To dau. Peggy Richards, wife of John Richards. Deeds of gift of negroes to each. To be admitted immediately to record. Document is called Deeds of gift and Testament.

JOHN WILKINSON of Wilkes Co. May 21, 1799; Nov. 3, 1806. To my children, all my property: To son Francis Wilkinson, a negro named Glass; Samuel, a negro Rachael; to dau. Ann Harrison, a negro Amy; To son, Pleasant Wilkinson, a negro Will; to son Bailey, a negro Silvey; to dau. Polly Wilkinson, a negro Sal; also other gifts to each. Legacy to son Sherard (Sherwood?). To son Jesse, negroes Ben and Cerena; to son Nathaniel, a negro Paul and bay mare. Exrs: Hazelwood Wilkinson,

Wm Jackson Wife Ellender
son John Jackson
Wm; Thomas; Henry

Bailey and Samuel Wilkerson. Wit: Thomas Grant, A. Keeling. Codicil: Gifts to son Francis Wilkinson. All other estate to be sold and divided. Wit: Peter Payner, Thomas Grant. Date Apr. 3, 1802 (codicil). Recorded in Will Book HH, pg. 17. Thos. Grant was finally acting executor.

JOHN COLLEY of Wilkes Co. Nov. 21, 1815; Nov. 21, 1815. It is my will and desire that there shall be a negro fellow purchased of the value of five hundred dollars for my son, France Colley, also gifts of horses and furniture. To son Spain Colley a negro fellow, furniture, horse, etc. To dau. Polly a negro Cheney and her two children, Cheney and Sophia, furniture and a horse. To dau. Louisa, my negroes Violet and Mary, horse and furniture, and cash. To dau. Betsy, similar gifts; my executors to purchase a negro for Betsy out of the money coming from the estate of my father-in-law in North Carolina. To dau. Nancy, similar gifts. Having given my son, Gabriel Colley his full share, he is to be paid only $300 at death of my wife. To granddau. Lucinda C. Tindall, the dau. of Betsy, legacy. Exrs: Son, France, and David Terrell. Wit: Job Callaway, David Terrell.

JOHN SCOLES. Aug. 18, 1819; Nov. 6, 1820. To wife Rachael all estate. Mentions his three children: Robert, Many and James Scoles. Exr: Wife. Wit: Samuel Kelly, Thos. Hutchins, James Moore, Robert Grier.

CALEB SIMMONS. Oct. 29, 1833; Dec. 1, 1834. To wife Miriam. To children: Hulda, wife of Richard Anderson; Julia, wife of Frances Wilkinson, Frances, wife of William Mattox; David Simmons; Sabrina Billingslea, wife of James Billingslea; sons Caleb and James Madison Simmons; Mitchell Taylor Simmons, a minor. Exr: Wm. Mattox. Wit: William Bowen, Jesse Simmons, Jesse M. Simmons.

RICHARD WOODRUFF. Feb. 26, 1835; July 12, 1836. To my son-in-law, Moses Sutton, who married my dau. Lotty, for the use of William and James Sutton, my grandsons. To John Flemister and his wife Hulda; to dau. Nancy Crawford; to my children Clifford Woodruff, and Matilda Reeves, wife of John D. Reeves. Exrs: Son, Clifford and son-in-law John D. Reeves. Wit: William Q. Anderson, Thomas Sutton. Codicil: Legacy to son Wyatt Woodruff. Provision for slaves. April 10, 1836.

GANAWAY MARTIN of Wilkes Co. July 24, 1819; Nov. 1, 1819. I have given to my daughter Sarah Thornton two hundred acres whereon the late Solomon Thornton lived. I have given my son William Martin 220 acres, which is his full share. I have given my son John Martin 200 acres, which is his full portion. To my son Henry Martin, notes and cash, which is in full of his share. To my son Austin Martin, after the decease of his mother and myself, the plantation and all improvements whereon I now live. To my dau. Elizabeth Webster, negroes, which is her portion. To my two daus. Frances Catchings and Nancy Catchings, cash. Exrs: James W. Jack,

Patrick J. Barnett, John Rorie, James Anderson, Recorded in Wills "HH", pg. 22.

GEORGE BAILEY. Sept. 23, 1819. To dau. Sydney Leverett one half the land I possess. To my gr. children, Feby Bailey, Peggy Dozier Bailey, George Reed Bailey, Polly Ann, and Josiah Bailey, the other half of my land at my death. Russell Bailey, trustee. To dau. Susannah Jennings, now Susannah Huddleston, her full part of land. To gr. dau. Elizabeth Bailey. To dau. Sydney Leverett, one third of the balance of my property, the other third to be divided among lineal heirs of Peggy Bailey, Feby and Peggy Dozier Bailey, George Reed Bailey, Polly Ann and Josiah Bailey. Russell Bailey, trustee, until they become of age. The other one third to be in care of Susannah Huddleston her life time, then to her lineal heirs. Exrs: Robert Leverett, George Huddleston, Russell Bailey. Wit: Thos. Greene, John Boxwell, Absolom Leverett. The Will was recorded in Oglethorpe Co., apparently. Found among Sup. Ct. Records, Wilkes Co., filed with original Wills, File "B".

GEORGE YOUNG, SR. dec. The will was recorded in the lost Book DD, pg. 143. Original papers reveal identity of heirs. John & George Young, Exrs. Appraisement Nov. 28, 1791. Heirs and legatees: Jesse Hodges, John Gibson, Zadock Barnard, Mary Gibson, James Young, Leonard Young. Dec. 17, 1792. Test: John Lumpkin. (Original papers, file Y)

MARY HAMRICK of Lincoln Co. May 14, 1817; Nov. 1, 1820. To son James Hamrick. To dau. Nancy Moncrief. To son Peter Hamrick. To dau. Frances Florence. To dau. Polly Hamrock. Gifts to Reuben Hamrick, Moses and Aaron Hamrick. All children to share equally. Mentions his plantation, etc. Francis Strother, Moses Hamrick, Exrs. Wit: John Quinn, William Quinn, Sr. Will Book HH, p. 41. Wilkes Co. Record.

WILLIAM MORRIS. Dec. 3, 1820; Jan. 9, 1821. To wife Ruth Morris all estate for life. At her death to be equally divided between Jacob Edwards, Wylie Acree, Mathew W. Vandivere, and Sarah Nelms. Exr: Wife, Ruth. Wit: John Rhodes, Redden Rhodes, Archibald Gresham. Will Book HH, p. 44.

WILKES COUNTY

Abstracts of Superior Court Cases from original loose papers, 1797 - 1850

The original documents are filed in Inferior Court Office (now Ordinary's Office). At the time these Superior Court documents were found in the attic and cellar of Wilkes County Courthouse no provision was made to file these papers in the Superior Court Office. These papers were salvaged and filed in Ordinary's Office and remain on file in that office.

JOSEPH ANTHONY, dec. In Equity. Anselm and Micajah Anthony againt heirs of Joseph Anthony, dec. Heirs: Wm. Stokes, the child of Mary, dau. of Joseph Anthony, dec: Augustus Anthony, (by his gdn. Wm. Robinson) the grand child of said Joseph, dec. his father, Joseph C. Anthony, now dead: Wm. Robinson and wife Elizabeth T., formerly widow of Joseph C. Anthony: Rhoderick Easley and wife Nancy, dau. of Joseph, dec. Petition for division. Jan. 21, 1831 FILE - ANTHONY

WILLIAM BARNES, dec. late of McIntosh Co., Nov. 19, 1810. Minors: William, Henry, Lucy Ann Barnes; widow Martha, now wife of Wm. DeLoney of Camden Co. "Lucy married Mr. Stewart, Nov. 17, 1810". FILE - BARNES

POUNCY BUNCH, dec. Chancery Court Bill for distribution, June 22, 1833. Judith Bowles of Wilkes Co., in 1823, bequeathed to Gideon Bowles and to Hannah Crews Bowles, orphans of Pouncy Bunch, property in Goochland Co., Va., and in Ga., now in possession of Sarah Bunch, widow of said Pouncy. FILE-BUNCH

BENJAMINE BORUM, dec. John B. Leonard, adm. James Borum was dead in 1820, leaving heirs: James Borum: Geo. W. Carter and wife Margaret, formerly Borum: (James and Margaret, minors): Elizabeth Borum, Margaret Borum the widow: Mary: Thomas and Edmund Borum. James lately was twenty one and is entitled to his share, Margaret Carter now is entitled to her share. Date of petition, 1833. FILE - BORUM

JOHN BEALL, dec. Joseph and Nathan Beall, exrs. In Equity: June 15, 1821. Heirs and distributees: John Beall: Elizabeth Dozier, Richard Dozier, her husband: Harriett Harding, her husband, John H arding; Rachael Pounds, her husband, Garrett Pounds: Mary Brown, her husband George A. Brown: and Lloyd A. Beall. Petition: That John Beall died testate in 1803, naming wife Mary and two children, Polly and Lloyd, otherwise Floyd: that the widow died in 1820. FILE - BEALL

EDWARD BLACK, dec. Will, 1797, names four daughters. Lydia died: the court gave her share to Edward Black and Stephen Williams; John McKenzie of Warren Co. signs quit claim to his share in right of his wife.

FILE - BLACK

1833 George Bailey dec.
John Bell and wife Phoebe Bailey dec. 1830 and wife Polly Ann Bailey
Wilkes, GA

WM. F. BOOKER, dec. Bill In Equity, Feb. 1810. William F. Booker married daughter of Robert Moore of Sumner Co., Tenn: that Wm. M. Booker died; Jesse Clark, adm. against Joshua Morgan, Thomas F. Booker et al. Interogatory: Did Wm. Moore make deed to Wm. M. Booker, the grandson of said Moore? Answer. I knew Wm. F. Booker before he married and I was brother-in-law to Wm. F. Booker. I heard Wm. F. Booker mention property of his son Wm. M. Booker had from his gr. father, by his (Wm. F's) brother Gideon Booker which was land in Greene Co., in 1794. Jane Carter, wife of Charles Carter, states Wm. F. Booker married her sister, etc. Thomas F. Booker now claims certain negroes of est. of Wm. F. Booker, dec.
FILE - BOOKER

GEORGE BAILEY, dec. John Bailey and wife exrs. Robert Leverett, now of Upson Co.; John Bell and wife Phoebe, formerly Bailey; Polly Ann Bell formerly Bailey who married said John Bell after death of first wife Phoebe Bell, in 1830; George Bailey, gr. father of Phoebe Bailey Bell, first wife of said John Bell; and Polly Ann Bell, formerly Bailey; the said gr. father bequeathed unto his gr.children Feby Bailey, George Reed Bailey, Polly Ann Bailey, wife of said John Bell, and Josiah Bailey one half of his lands, to be in care of Russell Bailey till they come of age. Petition by heirs June 22, 1833. Remark: The will of gr. father George Bailey is recorded in Oglethorpe Co.
FILE - BAILEY

JOHN COOK, dec. Robert Buckner and wife Elizabeth Mabry against Joseph and Benjamine Cook and Wm. Stubblefield, April 1797. That John Cook,gr. father of Elizabeth Mabry, died in 1780 and left will devising many slaves to said Elizabeth, and her sister Polly, sicne dead.
FILE - COOK

COATS, DRUCILLA, dec'd. In Equity June 1830. Drucilla died in 1826 leaving as her only heirs John D.Coats, and Nancy Harris, lately dead; Fanny Eidson who married Thomas R. Eidson; Elizabeth Cain, formerly Coats, the intestate of Newton Cain, David Barron, gr-son of said Drucilla, whose mother died before death of Drucilla; and after death of Drucilla, John B. Leonard, Sr. was appt. gdn. of said Elizabeth; Fanny Eidson died leaving Thomas R. Eidson, her husband, and several children; that Leslie Coats died and had not been paid his share of estate of Drucilla, dec'd. Petition by the heirs: Peter Harris, John D. Coates, Newton Cain. Bill in Equity, Mch. 16, 1827, that Drucilla died leaving another dau. Sallie who married Samuel Barron; Sallie died leaving child David Barron.
FILE - COATS

HUGH CRUTCHER, dec. Heirs of Crutcher against John T. Graves, adm. Bill for Distribution, 1825. Charles Fouche and wife Lucy; Sarah Fouche, widow of John Fouche; Coleman Crutcher; Robert Crutcher; Susannah Ficklin, all children of Hugh Crutcher, dec.; William Gordon who married Elizabeth Snead? Who also was the dau of Hugh Crutcher; Wm. Crutcher, son of said Hugh, dec: Henry Crutcher, brother of Hugh, dec.
FILE - CRUTCHER

BENJAMINE CATCHINGS Estate. In Equity. Ann Arnett, admr. of Mrs.

Mildred Carlton, relict of said Benj. Catchings, against the heirs of said Catchings: Joseph and John Catchings of Mississippi, John McNeil and wife, Matilda Catchings McNeill, Seymore Catchings of Putnam Co., Ga., Ann Bird, Oliver C. Arnett of Wilkes Co. That Benj. Catchings died in 1798; that Mrs. Mildred C. Carlton died in 1840. FILE - CATCHINGS

GEORGE CLORE. Original deed of gift to children: Abner, Anna, Abi, Able, Abram and Asa Clore, Jan. 11, 1808. FILE - CLORE

THOMAS DARRACOTT, dec. In Chancery. That Thomas Darracott died the latter part of the last century, intestate, and left children: Frances is dead, no issue: John Darracott is dead and left issue, some are living: Mary Darracott married John Wingfield, who died before Elizabeth: Benj. Borum married Peggy or Margaret Darracott; now Benjamine is dead, and that Peggy died before Elizabeth Darracott: Elizabeth Darracott died without heirs, and the said Elizabeth first married John Terrell and lived to advanced age and left no heirs and that she married John Terrell with consent of her Mother. Bill for investigation, Aug. 1838. FILE - DARRACOTT

THOMAS DRAPER, Sr., dec'd. State of Tenn., Smith Co. Thomas Draper Jr. Against Joel Sutton, Feb. 22, 1829. Deposition of David Hogue and Polly Cartwright in Tenn: "Lawson and Edward Draper are sons of Thomas Draper, Sr." FILE - DRAPER

THOMAS H. DIXON, dec'd. Petition by heirs: Martha R. Dickson, Thomas H. Dixon, Jr., both minor heirs; George B. and N. B. Dixon, Sarah Dixon, Marcus T. Dixon, minors of Thos. H. Dickson, dec. Mch. 3, 1838. FILE - DIXON

DARDEN DAVIS, dec. Samuel Brooks, admr. Interrogatory in 1827. Darden Davis came from Isle of Wight Co., Va. - had lived in Nansemond Co., Va. FILE - DAVIS

JOHN FLING, dec. In Chancery July 18, 1827. Warren S. Hudspeth, admr. of Kitty Hudspeth, his wife, against Joseph Henderson and John Boren, exrs. Petition recites that John Fling, Father of Kitty Fling, wife of Warren S. Hudspeth, died testate about January 1816, the will naming children: Kitty, Thomas, John, Daniel and Jasper Fling and the said John Fling's widow Anna married Charles Smith and that in 1826, Warren S. Hudspeth married the said Kitty in 1816.
FILE - FLING

WILLIAM GIDDENS dec'd. Francis Giddens admr. In Equity. Jesse Everette and wife Rachael, dau. of said decedent and Francis Giddens, Jr. Co-heirs. May 2, 1816. FILE - GIDDENS

BARNARD HEARD, dec. John Heard, adm. Interrogatory: Dec. 1804. Did Barnard H eard let his sister Bridget have a negro Hannah? Elizabeth Walton said she knew Barnard Heard let his sister Bridget have Hannah. Application was made to Col. Stephen Heard, brother of Barnard, and Stephen said: Barnard's son John is admr. that John could give infor-

Elizabeth Allen 1823 m. Horn Greene ?

David Jackson and wife Sarah Horn Jackson

mation. Remark: Barnard's son John, living in 1804. He therefore was not the John who died in 1803, as has been claimed.
FILE - HEARD

JAMES HAY, dec'd. Gilbert and Charles Hay admrs. Thomas Stone, et al. against administrators: Thomas Stone married Mildred, the widow of said James Hay and that he was gdn. of Thomas, Melissa and Elizabeth Hay, orphans of said James Hay, dec. FILE - HAY

NANCY LEE, dec'd. Noah Lee, adm. Petition Dec. 8, 1828 by John Horn, Sr., gdn. of John Horn, Preston Horn, Silas Burns and wife Nancy Horn Burns, David Jackson and wife Sarah Horn Jackson, Polly Horn and Amelia Horn, all children of Sallie Horn, formerly Lee; that Sallie Lee married John Horn who later was father of children mentioned; that John Horn, Sr., died about 1820; Nancy Lee died 1822. Bill for division, 1824. FILE - LEE

THOMAS LASLEY, dec'd. R, Booker and Catherine Lasley admrs. Loyd Bell and wife Mary Lasley against Catherine Lasley, widow of Thomas, dec. and her children: Mary Lasley; Sarah who married Thomas Holliday; David Laslie of Greene Co.; Felix Lasley of Harris Co.; Thomas and Medium Lasley, all heirs of Thomas Lasley, dec. Bill of Complaint, Jan. 17, 1832. FILE - LASLEY

ALLEN MABRY, dec'd. Petition, Feb. 1840 that he married Nancy a dau. of James Sherrer who died in 1815 or 16, and James Sherrer now of Troup Co. and William Sherrer now are exrs. That Nancy has not received her full share. FILE - MABRY

JOHN MONTFORD, dec'd. James Montford, adm. Petition Aug. 1, 1809: John died, 1804. Four children: Theodrick, Harriett, and John, a minor. Elizabeth died. Admr. explains he used the proceeds for benefit of widow and children. FILE-MONTFORD

JOHN MOSS, dec'd. John S. Moss and Mark Anthony admrs. Bill for distribution Mch. 1847. Heirs: Joseph M.Gartrell and wife Sarah the widow of John Moss, dec'd; a daughter who married Daniel H. Standard; John S. Moss; and two minor children. John Moss died in 1846. Estate valued at $50,000.00. FILE - MOSS

LUCY MURPHEY, dec'd. Case in Equity, Jan. 15, 1851, Amanda Thornton, dau. of Lucy dec. in 1835; she married John Thornton by whom she had seven minor children: Thomas T., Samuel, James, Martha, Anderson, Solomon, and that Lucy Murphey of Wilkes Co., widow and mother of Amanda M. Thornton died Aug. 23, 1850, and left will. Amanda now refers to her Mother as Mrs. Lucy Simpson. FILE -MURPHEY

THOMAS MURRAY, dec'd. Sarah Murray adm. of estate of said Thomas Murray was now on Mch. 1, 1813. Sarah Johnson who made returns signed by Sarah Murray Johnson: Paid Hendon's sister Lucy Freeman her share. Paid Sally Hendon's share. FILE - MURRAY

WILLIAMS MATHIS dec'd. Copy of will exhibited in Wilkes Co. Court but recorded in Putnam Co. Date of will, June 4, 1816; proved Mch.

6, 1820. Mentions wife Winifred. To daus: Mary Ringo, Anna Flinn. Legacy to heirs of Elizabeth Bird. Residue to be divided among James Mathis, Robert, William, Nathaniel, Polly and Nancy Ringo. Legacy to Sally and Margaret Williamson. Thomas and William Mathis, exrs. James Mathis of Limestone Co., Ala., formerly of Wilkes Co., states he is an heir of William Mathis, dec., that after the death of Winifred (widow) he appt. Charles Smith to receive his share. Case, July 9, 1833. FILE - MATHIS

JOHN POPE, dec'd. Thomas Wooten, William Johnson, admrs. In Chancery, Aug. 1828. Demurer: John Pope died leaving legatees: Thomas J. Pope, Tabitha Thurmond, Henry Pope, Martha Walker, formerly Pope, now wife of Wm. Walker: Dolly Riddle who married Anderson Riddle; Nancy who married Gilford Cade; Sarah Pope who married James M. Anderson, Kidda Pope the widow. FILE - POPE

ANN PRAY, dec'd. Petition by heirs: Jane M. Charlton, Phoebe M. Douglas, wife of Thomas Douglas, formerly Phoebe M. Charlton; Harriett F. Jackson, wife of Jesse Jackson; Sarah and Mary Pray Charlton, children of Francis Charlton, - all legatees of Ann Pray, July 1835. FILE - PRAY

JOHN PETEET, dec'd. John R. Peteet, adm. In Equity. Case against Elizabeth Peteet, adm. of John R. Peteet, dec., who was admr. of John Peteet, Sr. dec. Interrogatory held in DeKalb Co. John Peteet testifies on trial that Richard Peteet his father had given each of his gr-sons a negro,(who were named for him) and that John R. Peteet is a grandson of Richard Peteet and was named after him (John Richard Peteet). Testamony relates to ownership of a negro boy Tyson. Case, Aug. 5, 1847. FILE-PETIT

THOMAS C. PORTER, dec., Augustus W. Flynt, adm. Superior Court, Aug. 24, 1846. Administrator against the heirs who are all cousins, of Thos. C. Porter, dec'd., maternal and paternal heirs: James H. Flynt; Amelia C. Jones; Michael S. Shehan and Virginia his wife, all of Wilkes Co., George W. Flynt of Taliaferro County and Augustus W. Flynt who are children of Sarah Porter, aunt of Thomas C. Porter, dec., sister of Thomas C. Porter's father: Fayette Porter of Ala.: Henry B. Porter of Ala.: Charles H. Porter of Talbot Co., Ga. and Sarah Reese of Columbia Co. Ga., who are children of Charles Porter, a brother of Thomas C. Porter's father, likewise, cousins: Solon N. Porter, Benjamine F. Willis and Martha his wife, and the children of Augustus Walker whose names are Mary, the wife of Charles Gartrell; Frances Porter, wife of Oliver Stanford; Edny, wife of Jeremiah Gafford of Stewart Co., who died since decease of Thos. C. Porter, and who with Solon and Martha were children of Thomas Porter, a brother of Thomas C. Porter's father: George W. and James P. H. Porter of Tenn.; the children of Nicholas Porter, another brother of Thomas C. Porter's father; Robert R. Randolph and Mariah Randolph of Wilkes Co.; Henry Randolph of Bibb Co.; Martha Triplett of Florida; Thomas R. Randolph of Fla., Thomas Hamilton of Columbia Co., children of sister of Thos. C. Porter's Mother. Aug. 2, 1846. FILE - PORTER

JOHN QUERNS, dec. John Spear, exr. Bill in Equity, Jan. 14, 1817.

1797
William Simmons
sons: Willis
Solomon
John
Henry
Asa

Petition by Heirs: John Spear: William and Samuel Arnett; Nancy Anders, formerly Arnett; Mary Stephens, formerly Arnett; Margaret Anderson formerly Arnett; the children of Mrs. Ann Arnett who was the sister of John Spear, half brother of John Querns, dec. See John Quern's will. Wilkes Co. FILE - QUERNS

RICHARD REYNOLDS, dec. Joseph Henderson and Thomas Reynolds, admr. Receipts by heirs: Thomas Matthews, Wm. Barker, David Thrash, Richard Reynolds by his gdn. Estate settled by admr. with will annexed. Numerous heirs. Mch. 1801. FILE - REYNOLDS

RICE, --? March 1801. Heirs Receipts: Nancy Rice, Mary Stanley, by their gdn. Joseph Shelton: Benjamine Higgason, Charles, Stanley. Signed in Louisa Co., Va. Name of decedent not given in this record. FILE - RICE

WILLIAM SIMMONS to his sons. Original deed of gift, 1797, Sons: Willis, Solomon, John, Henry and Asa Simmons. FILE - SIMMONS

CHARLES SKIPWORTH, dec. In Chancery. Fulver Skipworth, adm. in Baton Rouge, La.: Letters of administration granted in Chatham Co., Ga. Mch. 1818. A. Semmes, admr. in Wilkes Co. The deceased left legacy to his Mother, Mrs. Lucy Corbin, "Sur named" Lapoule Dauberming, who resided in Martinique, France, or French, West Indies. Copy of Will and letter in French filed in Wilkes Co. FILE - SKIPWORTH

THOMAS J. TAIT of Wilkes Co. died in 1829. Petition by heirs: Augustine D. Statham and Lucy, his wife, formerly Tait. Paschal D. Klugh and wife Martha (Tait) of S. C.; Tavener W. Fortson of Elbert Co. who married Catherine Tait, who died leaving a child; Permelia Tait, Zemri W. Tait, Lawrence P. Tait, Sarah Y. Riddle, Case, Feb. 1831 FILE - TAIT

PERNAL TRUITT, dec. Bill in Equity, July 1843. David Montgomery and wife Sarah (Truitt); Nancy Collins, formerly Truitt, widow and relict of Eli Collins, the said Eli died previous to death of Purnal Truett, Sr.; John Martin and wife Martha (Truitt); Isaac Martin and Mary B. Truitt, the said Martha and Mary being the only heirs of Riley Truett Sr., late of Wilkes Co.; the said Purnal Truett, Sr. died about Nov. 12, 1833. Superior Court record. Inferior Court record gives names of heirs residing out of Wilkes Co.; Sarah Truitt, relict of John Truitt; Frances Shaw and husband Watson Shaw; James m. Truitt; Delphia Spears and husband, Joshua Spears; Sarah Spears and husband Jefferson Spears; Elizabeth, Alfred, Nathan, Martha, Indiana Truett; Purnal Collins, adm. of Eli Collins; Amended Bill signed by Inferior Court Clerk, Oct. 21, 1843. Newspaper clipping attached to original Bill in Equity. FILE - TRUETT

BENJAMINE THURMOND, dec. Micajah, Philip and James Thurmond adms. In Equity. Nine distributees: James, Philip, Thomas and Benjamine Thurmond, a minor; Sarah Thurmond who married Philip Moss; Polly Thurmond who married Philip Thurmond; Nancy Thurmond who married Wm Thurmond: Elizabeth who married Wm. Overstreet, Judah who married Francis McLendon, who is now gdn. of Benj. Thurmond, Oct. 1807. Writ of Partition, Dec. 2, 1815 also Fi Fa in favor of Robert Sayer against Philip Thurmond, 1812, on 100 acres bequeathed by will of Wm. Thurmond to Philip Thurmond. FILE - THURMOND

ELIZABETH THOMAS, dec. Page 161. Chancery Court Case 1849, gives names of other distributees and places of residences: Mark Williams; Wm. Coats; James Hawkins and wife Sarah, a great niece ; Emily E. Smith, Mother of Eleanor Crain who was Mother of Burton Crain, Eleanor, Warren, Joel E. and Wm. H. Crain; Wm. M. Marks and wife Catherine; John H. Marks, Sr., Mark Williams; SamuelB. Marks and wife Louisa; Nicholas Thompkins, Mary Cargile and O. K. Kennon. Heirs residing outside of Wilkes Co. Wm. Coats of Ala.; John Thompkins of Baker Co., Ga.; Nicholas Thompkins of Heard Co., Ga.; Mary Cargile of Butts Co., Ga.; Owen H. Kenan and wife Martha H. of Murray Co., Ga.; Nicholas M. Marks of Ala.; the Crain heirs of Arkansas; and the children of Susan Pinkard or their gdn. 1849. FILE - E. THOMAS

GEORGE WILLIS, dec. Robert J. Willis, adm. Willis R. Callaway's receipt for his wife's share in six negroes, assigned to his wife (who was formerly the widow of George Willis, Jr. dec.) and to Richard W. Willis son of George Willis, dec'd. Feb. 1, 1845. FILE - WILLIS

JOHN WALKER, dec. James Walker, Thos. Wootten, admrs. Writ of Partition, Mch. 28, 1828. Distributees: Wm. Q. Anderson in right of his wife Sophia; sons, Robert Walker, James, Richard G., John S. Walker; James Meriwether Walker, and Wm. Walker, minors of Wm. Walker, dec., the son of John Walker, dec. FILE - WALKER

RICHARD B. WOOTTEN, dec. John Pope and James Cade, adms. George H. Hughes and wife Anith against administrators. Petition Jan. 1816. That George H. Hughes married Anith, dau. of said dec., who died in 1797, leaving widow Lucretia who married Fielding Thurmond and had five children, including Arnith whose gr. father, Nathaniel Jones of N. C. sent for Arnith who had lived in N. C. many years; she has not received her full share. FILE - WOOTTEN

MIDDLETON WOODS, dec. In Equity, Feb. 28, 1821, Distributees: Josiah Woods, brother of said Middleton dec.: Robert Woods, Sr., Father of said Middleton, dec.: Francis Hill and wife Elizabeth, sister of Middleton, dec.: Robert Woods, Jr., William Woods, John Woods, Bailey M. Woods, John H ale and wife Polly all being sons and daus. of Hugh Woods, dec.a brother of Middleton, dec: Citizen S. Woods and Robert T. Woods, Samuel Woods, Peter and George Wood (by Samuel Houston) Robert Houston and wife Elizabeth, all sons and daus. of John Woods, dec'd., a brother of said Middleton: Josiah W., Robert N. Dickinson, John Clay and wife Elizabeth, all children of John Dickinson and wife Isbel, dec. the said Isbel being sister of said Middleton, dec.: Thomas M. Henry and wife Nancy, George Philips & wife Polly, Reuben Wade and wife Lucy, being children of Hugh and Peggy Martin, dec., said Peggy being sister of Middleton, dec. Wilkes Co. Superior Court.
FILE - M. WOODS

Remarks: William and Middleton Woods, brothers, resided in Elbert Co., Ga. Partners in business. The two estates are of record in Elbert Co., Ga. Middleton's estate in probate book 1809 to 1812, p. 78.

Estate of brother William Woods, settlement recorded in "Minutes of Court 1791 to 1830" page 141. Elbert Co. Record - Numerous heirs mentioned were residents of Franklin Co., Va., also father, Robert Sr., living in Franklin Co., Va. in 1821. Reuben Woods lived in Madison Co. Terr. Miss. Dr. Geo. Philips, formerly of Oglethorpe Co., Ga. had settled in Dallas Co., Ala. Other heirs of Wm. Woods, including Middleton G. Woods and William H. C. Woods. FILE - WM. WOODS

DIVISION OF PROPERTY - DEEDS OF GIFT, ETC.
OFFICE OF SUPERIOR COURT CLERK
WILKES COUNTY, GEORGIA

- - - - -

JOSEPH ANTHONY and WIFE BETSY, of Wilkes Co. sell 536 acres on Fishing Creek, on James Anthony's line, to Mark and Bolling Anthony, with all appurtenances, thereto appertaining. July 14, 1793. Test: Bedford Brown, J. P. Deeds PP. page 151. Remark: Superior Court records recite that Joseph was a brother of Micajah Anthony, who was dead by 1794. Joseph and Bolling, admrs.

JOSEPH ANTHONY, of Wilkes Co., adm. of estate of Micajah Anthony, dec., to Armistead Stokes, who is heir in right of his wife to one half of the estate of Micajah, dec., and guardian of Micajah Anthony, the only child of said Micajah, July 20, 1809. Test: Bolling Anthony, Thos. Anderson. Deeds XX p. 383. (It is evident that Armistead Stokes married the widow of Micajah Anthony, dec.)

JOSEPH ANTHONY to son Mark Anthony, of Wilkes Co., and to son Micajah Anthony, of Elbert Co., valuable gifts. Sept. 3, 1809. Deeds YY-p.135

JOSEPH ANTHONY to son Micajah Anthony, of Elbert Co. and to son Anselm Anthony, of Wilkes co. Sept. 3, 1809, Deeds YY, p. 134

JOSEPH ANTHONY, SR. to son Joseph Anthony, Sept. 3, 1802. YY, p.133-138 Remark: Joseph, Jr. is recorded, Joseph Clark Anthony, later. Numerous Anthony deeds are available.

JOSEPH BURKS to his grandchildren: Gibson Barton, Caroline Barton, Elizabeth Ann Matilda Barton, Martha Washington Barton, Fanny Barton, Clary Fortune Barton, the children of my son-in-law Larkin Barton, who married my dau. Lucy. Feb. 14, 1824. Deeds HHH, p. 395.

JAMES BIBB to his children: Sally, Lucy, Polly, Elizabeth, Martha and James Bibb. Gift Sept. 6, 1792, Deeds II, p. 55

MILLY BENTLEY, widow of Daniel Bentley, late of Lunenburg Co., Va. in

Hammock

1792, Hugh Hammock, adm. Chancery Court, 1811, Lununburg Co., Va. Statement that Daniel and Mildred had three children: John H. Bentley, Robert H. Bentley, of Wilkes Co., Ann Bentley. Nov. 1815, Wilkes Co. Deed CCC, p. 42.

WM. BANKS to dau. Polly Perkins, of Smith Co., Tenn. 1819. Deeds FFF p. 202.

JOB CALLAWAY, SR. to son Jacob Callaway. Apr. 4, 1803. Deeds UU, p.145

JACOB CALLAWAY to his children: Susannah, Barham, Parker, Lavinia, Seaborn and Drury Callaway, all children of said Jacob. Dec. 9, 1803. Deeds UU, p. 146

JACOB CALLAWAY to son Parker Callaway, Jan. 4, 1817. Deeds BBB, p. 298

JOSEPH CALLAWAY, SR. to son Joshua and to sons Luke, Jesse and Woodson Callaway, 1817. Deeds FFF, p. 98

JOSEPH CALLAWAY, SR. to daus. Mary and Elizabeth Callaway, 1817. Deeds FFF, p. 102, 103.

JOSEPH CALLAWAY to son Jesse Callaway, 1819. Deeds FFF, p. 97

CALLAWAY: Numerous records.

CARLTON, LUCY - widow and adm. of Henry Carlton, dec. of Wilkes Co. conveys land to Isaac Carlton, Dec. 24, 1818: quit claim signed by heirs of decedent: Stephen, Joshua, Isaac L. Carlton, Robert W. Carlton, Rebecca Carlton, Thomas Carlton. Deeds GGG, p. 56, 57

JOSEPH CAULK and wife ABIGAIL, of Rutherford Co., Tenn. appt. son James Patterson Caulk, power of atty. to represent them in Wilkes Co. 1818. Deeds EEE, p. 329.

PHILIP COMBS to John Eidson, 1798, Deeds RR, p. 224
PHILIP COMBS, SR. to son Enoch Combs, 1810. Deeds YY, p. 367
PHILIP COMBS, SR. to son Philip Combs, Jr., 1810. Deeds YY, p. 230

JOHN CAIN to dau. Jane Waters of Oglethorpe Co., 1806. Deeds XX, p. 93

ELIJAH CLARK (General) to Jesse Thompson, gift, 1794. Deeds LL, p. 28
ELIJAH CLARK to Chas. Williamson, 1794. Deeds LL, p. 26
ELIJAH CLARK to Benajah Smith, gift, 1794. Deeds LL, p. 21

ROGER CASEY to Hannah Casey, 1793. Deeds LL, p. 80
ROGER CASEY to John Casey, 1792. Deeds II, p. 380
ROGER CASEY to Peggy Casey, 1792. Deeds II, p. 379
ROGER CASEY to Hannah Casey, 1792. Deeds II, 378
ROGER CASEY to Eleanor Casey, 1792. Deeds II, p. 377
ROGER CASEY to Sarah Casey, 1792. Deeds II, p. 377

CHARLES DEAN to Burket Dean, gift, Feb. 22, 1795. Deeds MM, p. 404
CHARLES DEAN to son Nathaniel Dean, 1795. Deeds MM, p. 404
CHARLES DEAN to son John Dean, 1795. Deeds MM, p. 405
CHARLES DEAN to son George Dean, 1794. Deeds MM, p. 407
CHARLES DEAN to Charles Smith, 1795. Deeds MM, p. 377

MOLLY DAVIS, of Wilkes Co., and Barnett Jeter, Exrs. of estate of AUGUSTINE DAVIS, sell 200 acres in Wilkes Co. to David Roberts of Persons Co., N. C., land originally granted to heirs of Augustine Davis Davis, dec. 1788. Deeds LL, p. 148. The balance of the land of A. Davis fell in Lincoln Co. when cut from Wilkes Co. in 1796. Deeds LL, p. 148. Identity of heirs are revealed from Lincoln Co. deeds. The will of A. Davis was lost in Book DD, Wilkes Co.
JAMES DOZIER, Robert Harris, Thomas Staples, John Saggus of Wilkes Co., William Dodson, David Vaughn, Benj. Hardin of Columbia Co., Sherrod Roberts, Jacob Hogue, James Hardin, Wm. Berry, Gdn. of Judith Staples Richard Dozier, adm. of Leonard Dozier, dec. of Warren Co. of the one part to Sherrod Little, land on Little River on the line of Stephen Staples, dec., Nov. 19, 1818. Deeds GGG, p. 41.

HEIRS OF JOSIAH ELLINGTON, JR., dec., sign agreement Jan. 19, 1819: Elizabeth M. Ellington, widow of decedent, John Wilson, Simeon Ellington, Hezekiah Ellington, James Chivers, Springer Gibson, Nancy Daniel, Cunningham Daniel, atty. for heirs of said Josiah. Deeds FFF, p. 76

THOMAS GRANT, now of Jasper Co., Ga. to Wm. B. Moore, John R. Moore, Mary Moore, children of Thomas Moore, all of Wilkes Co., certain negroes Apr. 8, 1818. Test: Luke Turner, Wm. Grant. Deeds EEE, p. 98

Heirs and distributees of JAMES GRAVES, dec.: Sarah Graves, adm., Robert C. Graves, Wm. Davidson (parent and gdn. of James, Jane, Sarah, Ellinor, Harriett, Hannah, John and Wm. Davidson), Littleton McKey, John Nesbit, of the one part to Thomas Simmons land in Wilkes Co. Signed: Robert C. Graves, Wm. Davidson, Littleton McKey, John Nesbit, Peggy Graves, wife of Robert C. Graves, Sarah Nesbit, wife of John Nesbit, Hannah McKey, wife of Littleton McKey. Dec. 3, 1818. Deeds EEE, p. 159

Heirs and legatees of OWEN GRIFFIN and ANNE, his wife, dec., late of Wilkes Co. to Owen Griffin, one of the heirs. Sale of land in Wilkes Co. Heirs: Joseph Griffin and Joseph Griffin for Anselm Cunningham, Wm. Heard, John Wright, Pleasant Pullen for children of Elisha Lay, Drury Griffin. Dec. 1822. Deeds HHH, p. 89.

EZEKIEL HARRIS to dau. Mary Evans, Letter Apr. 1805. Recorded May 5, 1820. Deeds FFF, p. 129

MARY HUGHES, widow of WILLIAM HUGHES, Barnard H. Hughes, Williamson Woodall, James Heard, Malcome A. Johnson, Wm. Hughes, heirs and distributees of Wm. Hughes, dec., sell land to Hartwell Jackson, Feb. 5, 1821. All parties of Wilkes Co. Deeds FFF, p. 44

JOHN HINTON to dau. Fathy Caroline Hinton, 1823. Deeds HHH, p. 74
JOHN HINTON to dau. Eliza Hinton. Apr. 10, 1820. Deeds HHH, p. 74.
JOHN HINTON to dau. Sophia Hinton, 1823. Deeds HHH, p. 75.

1807 Heirs of Drury Jackson sell to Hartwell Jackson
Heirs: George Muse
John Jackson
Wyche Jackson
Edmond Jackson
Wm Thomas
Greene Jackson

JAMES HAYS, gifts to his children: James, Allen and Mary Ann Hays, lands in Habersham Co., Mch. 6, 1824. Deeds HHH, p. 274

MARGARET HEARD, widow and relict of CHAS. HEARD, SR., dec., to my grandchildren: Margaret Heard, John G. Heard, Barnard H eard, the children of John G. Heard, gift of a negro Peg, Jan. 7, 1802. Deeds TT, p. 156

JOHN G. HEARD to son Barnard Heard, Feb. 22, 1812. Deeds YY, p. 410-11.
JOHN G. HEARD to all my children: Barnard Heard, Jane Germany Heard, Fanny B. Heard. Feb. 22, 1812. Deeds YY, p. 427

JAMES HINES, SR., of Greene Co. (Will) to my sons John Hines, James Hines, Elias Hines: To dau. Elizabeth Williams, gifts. Separate lands to each child, and negro property. To my wife during life. Exrs. George Tuggle and son James. Aug. 26, 1807. Wit: John Payne Peter Tatom Williams. Deeds YY, p. 137, Wilkes Co.

STEPHEN JOHNSON to son Stephen Johnson, gift, 1805. Deeds YY, p. 250

GEORGE JOHNSON, dec. Quit Claim by heirs to 200 acres on waters of Clarks Creek: William Baber, Thomas, Susannah, Isobel, John, Stephen and Prudence Johnson, all of Wilkes Co. Dec. 25, 1819

★ HEIRS OF DRURY JACKSON sell land to Hartwell Jackson; a plantation on Fishing Creek and Newford Creek, whereon said Drury, dec., resided. Heirs: George Muse, John Jackson, Wyche Jackson, Edmond Jackson, William Thomas and Greene Jackson. Dec. 1807. Deeds XX, p. 520

THOMAS JARROL to dau. Melissa Jarrol. Apr. 27, 1820. Deeds FFF, p. 121

BENJAMINE HUBERT to James Hubert, Gift. 1792. Deeds II, p. 256
BENJAMINE HUBERT to dau. Viney Hubert, 1807. Deeds XX, p. 507
HIRAM AND BENJAMINE HUBERT convey to Vinya or Vinay Hubert land on Hardin's Creek waters, being the one third part of a tract from Benjamine Hubert to James, Moses and Hiram Hubert, yet to be divided. Oct. 19, 1813. Deeds ZZ, p. 212.

Heirs of JOHN HEARD, SR., Nov. 1809. Deeds PP. p. 208. John Heard, Jr., John Dyson and Michael L. Dent of Wilkes Co., heirs and representatives of John Heard, Sr. of the one part to John Graves of Wilkes Co., land on Mill ford of Fishing Creek, containing 10-7/10 acres being part of a tract originally granted John Heard, Sr. Signed: John Heard, John Dyson, Michael L. Dent. Test: Robert W. Collier, A. G. Walton, Jesse Williams. Plat shows additional land of estate of John Heard, dec.

WASHINGTON KENDALL late of Wilkes Co., died in 1820 leaving no issue. His father, Allenton Kendall; brothers Bartholomew, Allen and Lunsford Kendall; sister Nancy Kendall, who married Jeremiah McFleming, became his sold heirs. We convey to Allen Kendall, one of the heirs, the whole property being the wish of our father who died without a will. Aug. 8, 1827. In Court of Pleas, Granville Co., N. C., heirs relinquish claim to Allen Kendall. Deeds KKK, p. 186.

John Graves

Heirs of JOHN MCDOWELL, dec.: Barnard Kelly, Wm. McLin, Henry Dowdy, Sarah McDowell and Baptist McDowell to the heirs of James McDowell, viz: Thomas McDowell, Joseph and Margaret McDowell, legatees of James McDowell, land in Wilkes Co. on the waters of Long Creek, adj. the line of John McDowell, dec., July 20, 1800. Deeds RR, p. 420

PHILIP LEE, dec. (Estate) Some account given in Callaway deeds herein.

JOHN LAYSON, of Wilkes Co. to James Layson, Gift, Nov. 17, 1790. Oliver and Morgan Layson, test. Deeds MM, p. 37.

JOHN LAYSON of Laurens Co., S. C. to James M. Layson, of Laurens Co., S. C., Oct. 28, 1791, Gift of land in Wilkes Co. Deeds MM, p. 38

NATHANIEL MCCOY, OF WILKES Co. to grandsons: John Flynt, Benjamine Flynt, William and Jasper Flynt; to my dau. Sarah D. Flynt. Aug. 10, 1822. Deeds HHH, p. 176

PETER MCLAUGHLIN, of Wilkes Co., to son, Thomas D. McLaughlin, furniture, horses, farm produce. Dec. 20, 1797.
(George, David and Betty McLaughlin mentioned as residents of Oglethorpe Co., set off from Wilkes Co. 1793). Deeds FFF, p. 347-241

JOSHUA MABRY to Jamison, Allen, Walton and Daniel Mabry gift of the plantation whereon said Joshua Mabry lives. Dec. 4, 1807. Deeds XX,p. 512.

ZILPHA and JOHN MONCRIEF to my father and mother, Josiah and Elizabeth Moncrief, land on Hardins Creek waters where they now live. Feb. 7, 1816. Deeds BBB, p. 247

RICHARD MELEAR to dau. Fenton Starr, gift, 1812. Deeds YY, p. 618

JOHN MINTON to son Wm. Minton, 1806. Deeds XX, p. 118

JOHN OWEN, SR., ISABELLA AND MILDRED OWEN, Francis H. Oliver and Mary Oliver, of Granville Co., N.C. to brother DANIEL OWEN, of Wilkes Co., Ga., power of atty. to receive our share of the estate of our brother, Thomas Owen, dec., of Wilkes Co., Sept. 1820. John Owen of Smith Co., Tenn. being legal heir of Thomas Owen, dec. to Daniel Owen, power of atty. to receive his share of said estate in Wilkes Co. Thomas Anderson, of Chesterfield Co., Va., being legal heir of THOMAS OWEN, dec., signs quit claim and appoints Daniel Owen power of attorney. Sept. 12, 1820- Deeds GGG, p. 105.

NICHOLAS PORTER, to son Thomas Porter. Deeds II, p. 560. 1789

HEIRS OF JAMES PATTERSON, dec. sell to John W. Cooper, executor of Isabella Patterson, dec., who was adm. of John A. Patterson, all of Wilkes Co., of the other part 200 acres on Uptons Creek, Dec. 7, 1817. Signed by Ann Arnold, Henry Laughter, Samuel Walker, Margaret Patterson, Wm. Walker, James Walker, James P. Caulk, agt. for Jacob Caulk in right of his wife, Abigail Patterson. Deeds FFF, p. 74-75.

STOVALL POOL to dau. Mary W. Hudspeth, wife of Wm. Hudspeth. Feb. 2, 1826. Deeds III, p. 185

IGNATIUS RAINES, SR., IGNATIUS RAINES, JR. AND HENRY RAINES, now of Oglethorpe Co., formerly of Wilkes, sell land in Wilkes Co. to Stephen Johnson, 1816. Deeds DDD, p. 93 - CCC, p. 407

MARY ROAN, JESSE ROAN, WILLIS J. ROAN and Wm. Bennett, now of Morgan Co., sell land in Wilkes Co. to Elizabeth Miller. Deeds EEE, p. 124

Heirs and representatives of PETER STROZIER, SR., dec., sell lands lying in Wilkes Co., Dec. 18, 1800. Signed by heirs: John Strozier, Peter Strozier, Jr.; heirs of George Darden; Major Henderson; John Peteet; Wm. Lunsford; Acton Nesh. Deeds GGG, p. 82

NICHOLAS SHRUPTRINE to DANIEL SHRUPTRINE, gift, 1812. Deeds YY, p. 420-477
NICHOLAS SHRUPTRINE to ISRAEL SHRUPTRINE, 1812. Deeds YY, p. 615
NICHOLAS SHRUPTRINE to ISRAEL MILLER, Mch. 12, 1812. Deeds YY, p. 491
NICHOLAS SHRUPTRINE, et al, 1812. Deeds ZZ, p. 23
NICHOLAS SHRUPTRINE to Jno. Cheny. Deeds XX, p. 26

LUCRETIA STEPHENS, formerly Kelly, to dau. Fanny B. Goodyear, Nov. 1813. Deeds FFF, p. 366

JOHN SLACK, SR. to son Joseph Slack, Dec. 14, 1831. Deeds LLL, p. 243

JOHN SMITH to Charles, John and Lucy Smith, children of my dau. Mary Smith, wife of John Smith, of Wilkes Co. Feb. 22, 1793. Deeds MM,p.420

BENJAMIN SHERROD to his children, gift of 100 negroes to be jointly owned. Children: Felix A. Sherrod, Mary A. Sherrod, Frederick H. Sherrod, Samuel Sherrod. Apr. 5, 1819. Deeds EEE, p. 175

WILLIAM SIMMONS to his sons and daughters 200 acres on Clarks Creek. Children: Willis, John, Henry, Asa, Solomon, Polly, Nancy, Rachael, Celinda. June 5, 1798. Deeds NN, p. 115

The heirs of JOHN SPRINGER, dec.: John Houghton and wife Nancy, of Greene Co., sell and convey to William Springer, Lucinda Thornton Springer, orphans of John Springer, late of Wilkes Co.; whereas the said John Springer gave his dau. Susannah Springer a large tract of land in Pendleton Co., S. C., which now has reverted to the estate of said John Springer, dec., the said John Houghton and wife Nancy sell and convey all their interest in the tract of land in S. C. June 13, 1806. Deeds WW, p. 200

PRISCILLA SWANSON, widow, to her children: Thomas, John, Richard and Joel Swanson, Deed of gift of her whole property, not described. June 8, 1793. Deeds SS, p. 334

ANTHONY SEAL to dau. Rachael Graham, Dec. 4, 1792. Deeds MM, p. 110
ANTHONY SEAL to dau. Mildred Seal, Dec. 4, 1792. Deeds LL, p. 111
ANTHONY SEAL to son Robert Seal, 1792. Deeds LL, p. 109
ANTHONY SEALE to Mary Seale, gift, 1792. Deeds LL, p. 108
ANTHONY SEALE, SR. to Anthony Seale, Jr., 1792. Gift. Deeds LL, p.106
ANTHONY SEALE, SR. to dau. Ann Rhodes, (also gift to Eustis Rhodes) Dec. 1792, Deeds LL, p. 103

ANTHONY SEALE to Alexander Seale, gift, Deeds LL, p. 104
ANTHONY SEALE to Jarvis Seale, gift, 1792. Deeds LL, p. 111

JANE SALE of Wilkes Co., to son Leroy Sale and to his daughter, Nancy Sale, of Madison Co., Mississippi Territory, all my claim to the estate of my father, Joseph Dawson, now of Amhurst Co., Va., which is the third part of the said estate which may fall to me. April 6, 1816. Deeds BBB, p. 128

WILLIAM SANSOME, JR., of Maury Co., Tennessee, son of William Sansome, Sr., to the Bank of Ga., 1820. Deeds FFF, p. 184

DORREL N. SANSOME, son of Wm. Sansome, Sr. to the Bank of Ga., 1820. Deeds FFF, p. 186

ELIZABETH SANSOME, atty. for Wm. Sansome, Sr., to the Bank of Ga., 1820. Deeds FFF, p. 186

BENJAMIN TALIAFERRO, Dec. Division of the negro property, 1822. Heirs and distributees: Benjamine Taliaferro, Lewis and David M. Taliaferro, Thornton Taliaferro, Zachariah Taliaferro, a minor; Nicholas A. Watkins; David and Wm. McGehee, sons of Martha McGehee, formerly Taliaferro, by their agent, Abner McGehee; David Monroe in right of his wife Ann, formerly Ann Taliaferro; Joseph A. Greene in right of his wife, formerly Margaret B. Taliaferro. Eliza A. Taliaferro, widow and relect of Benj., dec. Deeds GGG, p. 178 - 182. (Taliaferro Co., Ga. was named in honor of Col. Benj. Taliaferro, of Wilkes Co.)

WARREN TALIAFERRO, Dec., Division of negro property, July 10, 1819. Distributees: To Peachy R. Gilmer in trust for minor children of said Warren, dec.: Lucy G. Taliaferro, Zachariah, Sally, Sophia Taliaferro; Nicholas Powers in right of his wife, Mary W. Powers, widow and relect of said Warren Taliaferro, dec'd; Thomas Rainey in right of his wife, Mary E., formerly Taliaferro. Record recites the division was made according to the last will of Warren Taliaferro (not found). Reference: Original papers Oglethorpe Co. Inferior Court. Warren Taliaferro first lived in Wilkes Co. Deeds YY, p. 299 give place of residence, Pendleton Co., S. C., 1811

MATTHEW TALBOT to Patty Young, 1801, gift. Deeds SS, p. 38

RICHARD TAYLOR to Nancy Todd, Wm. F. Taylor, Joseph Taylor, gifts. Dec. 29, 1813. Deeds EEE, p. 259

ELIZABETH TODD, widow of JOHN TODD, dec., late of Wilkes Co. Heirs and legatees of said John Todd: Elizabeth, the widow, James Todd, John Todd, Elizabeth Todd, Wm. Todd, John Hammock, Margaret Todd, sell and convey 268 acres of land on Clarks Creek of Long Creek, which said Jno. Todd, dec., died possessed of, to Joseph Todd, one of the legatees, Feb. 5, 1813. Deed EEE, p. 95

JAMES THURMOND, gift to his brother, Absolom Thurmond, Apr. 6, 1803. Deeds TT, p. 260

Heirs of JAMES TOLES, dec. to SUDDUTH TOLES, 1819. Heirs: Barsheba Toles, Frances Toles, Thomas Brown, in right of wife Lucy Toles, James Toles, Jr., Hannah Toles, Mary and Rebecca Toles. Sale of 180 acres on Newford Creek. Deeds FFF, p. 19

JOHN WHITLOCK to dau. Polly Jarroll, gift, 1794. Deeds LL, p. 72

Heirs of THOMAS WORTHAM, SR. and THOMAS WORTHAM, JR. of the one part to William C. Wortham; sale of 300 acres in Wilkes Co. Signed: G. W. Griffin for John Griffin, J. W. Bailey for Rose? Bailey, William Wortham, Lemuel Wortham. Nov. 22, 1822. Test: Thomas Gilmer, Deeds HHH, p. 157

GEORGE WOOTTEN to dau. Elizabeth Wootten, my plantation, 1802. Deeds UU, p. 209

WILLIAM WYLIE, dec., Estate. We relinquish our rights and title to all estate of Wm. Wylie, dec. on consideration of receiving our equal part of estate before the death of Wm. Wylie. Given under our hands and seal this 20th of Sept. 1786. Signed: Stephen Doss, George Gilmore, Hannah Gilmore, Humphrey Gilmore, Deeds RR, p. 240. A division of estate of Wm. Wylie, dec., young Elizabeth's share is left in care of her mother. One share to Adam Wylie, one share to James Wylie, one share to Jane Wylie, one share to Martha Wylie, a share (100 acres of land) to John Wylie. Apr. 14, 1799. Testator: Jesse Heard, ? Heard. Deeds RR, p. 240

JONATHAN WOODALL, of Wilkes, and his two brothers, John and James Woodall, of the one part to Etheldred Jelks, of the County of Greene, sell land whereon said Jonathan once lived, and from whence he lately moved. Jan. 10, 1800. Signed: Jonathan Woodall and wife Elizabeth, John Woodall, James Woodall, Etheldred Jelks. Deeds RR, p. 384

HETTY WELLS to son James Wells, 1819. Deeds FFF, p. 127

MICAJAH WILLIAMSON to dau. Polly Williamson, 1795. Deeds NN, p. 104 (Not named in her father's will)
MICAJAH WILLIAMSON, SR. to dau. Eliza Williamson, gift, 1795. Deeds NN, p. 106
MICAJAH WILLIAMSON, SR. to his son, Jefferson, 1795. Deeds NN, p. 115
MICAJAH WILLIAMSON to son Wm. Williamson, 1795. Deeds NN, p. 110 (Refer to will for names of other heirs)

GEORGE YOUNG and SUSANNAH to Geo. Young, Jr., 1790. Deeds HH, p. 107

GEORGE YOUNG, SR. to son Leonard Young, 1791. Deeds II, p. 78

ORDINARY'S OFFICE
INFERIOR COURT

DISTRIBUTIONS OF ESTATES

Abstracts are taken from Executors and Administrators Returns on Estates of record in the office of Judge of Inferior Court. For additional early probate records including wills, refer to Early Georgia Records, Wilkes County, Volumes 1 and 2. Compiled and published by Grace Gillum Davidson.

JOEL CHIVERS, dec., division of negro property, Nov. 1, 1819. Heirs: Elizabeth Chivers, the widow; Henry T. Chivers, Joel M. Shivers, Nancy L. Chivers, Frances E. Chivers, minors. Remark: Frances E. married her cousin, Thomas Holly Chivers, the poet-genius. Annual Returns 1816-22, p. 270

JACOB SLACK, dec., Jesse Slack and Wm. Andrews, adms. Jan. 10, 1824. Paid John Slack his share. Paid Jacob L. Slack, gdn. of Joseph Slack, the distributive share of said Joseph. Paid Jacob L. Slack his share. Paid Archibald Slack his share. Paid John Bentley, in right of his wife, his share.

JAMES FINLEY, dec., Samuel Finley, adm., Mch. 28, 1828. Paid Heirs: John Finley, James Finley, James Lysle, Isobel Finley, David Lawson. Returns 1820 to 1829. p. 174, 179. Same book pages 198, 201: David, Jane and William Finley mentioned as minors of said James, dec.

GEORGE BOSWELL, dec., Sarah Boswell, adm., June 7, 1825. Accts. of minors: Elizabeth, Johnson, Sarah, Jane H., Frances C. Boswell. Returns 1820-29, p. 3.

GEORGE FOUCHE, dec., William Slayton, adm., Mch. 2, 1829. Paid heirs: Mary Fouche, Ann Fouche, Thomas Fouche, Susannah Fouche, for William and George Fouche. Returns 1820-29, p. 373

FRANCIS GIDDENS, dec., Elizabeth Giddens, admr. Paid legatee, Taliaferro Jones, his share. Returns 1820-29, p. 228

WILLIAM GRANT, dec., Patrick Furley, exr., July 1, 1829. Paid legatees: A. B. Ragan's wife, Ann R. Grant, the share left her by will of Abram Simons. Returns Book 1820-29, p. 472

WILLIAM GRANT, dec., Dr. Wylie B. Ector, who is exr. in right of his wife Ketura Grant, formerly the widow of William Grant, Sr. Heirs mentioned in this record, Jan. 5, 1829: A. B. Ragan, in right of his wife Ann R. Grant; Thomas W. Grant; Augustine

L. Grant. Returns 1820-29, p. 390

JOHN WILKINSON, dec., Thomas Grant, adm., Dec. 9, 1826. Paid Legatees John Wilkinson, Bailey Wilkerson, Joseph Johnson, Vincent Harrison. Thos. Grant states to the court the heirs had scattered over 800 miles - that he can not settle the estate. Note: The will was signed 1799, proved in 1806. Returns: 1820-29, p. 314

MATTHEW TALBOT, dec., July 7, 1828. A large estate. Matthew endorsed for many persons, including business firms in Charleston and Augusta. Tax digest and other records indicate the estate was mainly lost. Identity of heirs are not readily found. Family records are available.

JAMES WILLIS, dec., Daniel Owen, gdn. of minors, July 5, 1825. Paid heirs and minors: James Willis, Francis Willis, Elizabeth Willis. Returns 1825-29, p. 7

SIMPSON MCLENDON, dec., Francis McLendon, gdn. Minors accts. July 2, 1827. Penelope, Martha and William McLendon. Returns 1825-29, p. 174

BOOK OF RETURNS 1819 to 1826

PLEASANT WILKINSON, dec., Jemima Wilkinson, gdn., July 6, 1819. Accts. of minors: Lavinia Wilkinson, Pleasant L., Joel Jabez and John Wilkinson, Jr., page 31. (Book of Returns 1828-31, p. 31 and 314)

MARY BARRETT, dec., John Spearman, adm., Mch. 25, 1822. Paid legatees: Nancy Barrett in full of the will of her grandfather: Permelia Barrett: Robert Barrett: Lewis Barrett in full of his grandfather's estate, of Gabriel Toombs, dec. Paid Robert Barrett in full of estate of grandfather, Gabriel Toombs, p. 227

JOHN GUNN, dec., David Pool, adm. in right of his wife. Minors: Leslie and George Gunn. May 6, 1825. p. 454

CHARLES HOFF, dec., Susannah Hoff, gdn., Mch. 4, 1822. Charles Hoff, Fanny, Ann and Susannah Hoff, minors. p. 215

JAMES LEE, dec., Daniel Lee and William Robinson, adm. Division Dec. 24, 1821. Heirs: John Lee, Peggy Lee, Hugh G. Lysle, William Lee, Joseph Lee. p. 370

JACOB HAMMONDS, dec., John Huguley, exr. Apr. 8, 1824. Paid guardian for five minors. p. 410

JOHN BURDINE, dec., Margarett Burdine, now wife of John Stroud, exr., with John Stroud. Nov. 1, 1819. p. 45

JOHN BURDINE, dec., Margaret Burdine, exr., with Reuben Scott (her husband) Mch. 1824. Devises: Thos. B. Danforth in right of his wife, Matilda Burdine, A.G. Norvell, George M. Burdine, Charles Burdine, Richard Burdine, p. 45. (remark: Sons Clarke and Reuben had been paid under terms of the will proved in 1816)

ACQUILLA BURROUGHS, dec., Joseph Jorden adm., Jan. 6, 1820. Division among heirs: Peggy Burroughs, widow: Abraham M. Matthews: Mary Burroughs, minor. p. 154

DAVID EVANS, dec., Arden Evans adm. Jan. 9, 1821. Paid distributees: John Bates, James Bates, Jesse Evans, Anderson Bates, Elizabeth Evans, William Evans, Peter Lunsford, who married Susannah Evans, John W. Bates, who married Rhoda Evans. Returns 1819-26, p. 133

DAVID ELLINGTON, dec., Henry F. Ellington, adm., also adm. of Mrs. Jane Ellington, dec. Returns Jan. 2, 1829. Paid Charles H. Ellington; paid Milly H. Ellington; paid Zachariah H. Darden; paid George H. Hanson, for heirs of Nathan Ellington; paid Wm. Ellington agent for Josiah Ellington; paid Francis Ellington for heirs of Nathan Ellington; paid H. P. Ellington; paid Daniel Dupree agent for John Ellington; paid Jorden Mabry, exr. of Jane Ellington, who was exr. of Daniel Ellington, in her life time. Paid John Hendricks; paid John Biggers; paid Frances Hamilton of Va.; paid Daniel Dupree. William Ellington had been paid. Statement: "There were twelve heirs". Returns 1820-29, p. 372-3

JOHN POPE, dec., Nov. 8, 1821. Division: Henry Jossey, James Matthews, Augustine B. Pope, Wylie Pope, Patsy (Martha) Pope, Rowena Pope, Thomas Henderson, who married Mary Pope 1820. Book of Appr. and Returns 1824-28, p. 26

JAMES WOOTTEN, dec., Thomas and Lemuel Wootten, exrs., Jan. 11, 1827. Distributees: Tabitha, James, Louisa, Francis, Lemuel, Gilbert Hay Wootten and Joel Wootten; Richard Sale in right of his wife Myra; Fielding Hinton in right of his wife Mary. Book of Appraisements and Returns, 1824-28, p. 249

JOHN LANGDON, dec., Isaac Langdon and William Robertson, admr. Heirs: William Robertson, Nancy Martin, Elizabeth Hawkins, Isaac Langdon,

West
Favor

Felix, Lewis and Catherine Davis, John Langdon, Mary Langdon (widow), Samuel Langdon. May 15, 1826. Book of Appr. and Returns, 1824-28, p. 168

SAMUEL WELLBORN, dec., no. admr.? Division Jan. 5, 1827. Heirs: Charles R. Greene, John W. Wellborn, Katherine C. Wellborn, Mrs. Wellborn, later Mrs. Jock. Returns 1828-31, p. 442

JOHN HARDEN FOSTER, dec., Division Mch. 19, 1823. Francis Foster, Eliza Foster, Charter Campbell in rights of his wife. Returns 1821-25, p. 89

"DAY BOOK" - 1830-1836 - Annual Returns

JOHN HEARD, dec., Dec. 3, 1832. Division of negroes: Elizabeth Heard, widow. Thomas Heard, James Heard, John Heard, Charles Heard, Mary Anne Heard, Alexander, Mark and Frances Heard, all children of John Heard, dec. p. 194

CHARLES MATTOX, dec., Division of Negroes, Jan. 9, 1832. Heirs: Jacob Johnston, Amelia C. Mattox, William Mattox. p. 49

THOMAS HEMPHILL, dec., Aaron A. Cleveland, gdn. Division. Heirs: Emily J. Hemphill, Cyrus T. Hemphill, Aaron A. Cleveland who married Nancy S. Hemphill. Jan. 6, 1836. p. 443

THOMAS GRANT, dec. Division of negroes, Jan. 3, 1831. Negroes in Jasper Co., Ga., devised by will of said Thomas Grant to heirs of William Grant, dec. Devises: A. R. Ragan, Augustine L. Grant, Thomas W. Grant, Eliza J. Grant., p. 205

JOHN M. WEST, dec., Dec. 1, 1831. Division of negroes. Heirs: John Thornton, Charles P. West, Seymore Catchings, Nancy Crooks West, Mary Ann West. p. 51

NELSON POWELL, dec., John B. Kendrick, gdn. Petition for division in part of John Kendrick in right of his wife, Sarah Ann Powell, Mch. 18, 1836. p. 430

ISAAC CALLAWAY, dec., John Barrett and Mary Callaway, exrs. Nov. 19, 1834. Agreement of legatees: Lewis B. Callaway; William A. Callaway; George W., James H., Eliza R., Merrit P., Harriet M. Callaway; H umphrey Tomlinson. p. 405

JOHN FAVER, dec., Dec. 31, 1830. Division of negroes among heirs: Obadiah Faver, Robert C. Daniel, John B. Faver, William A. Faver,

Sarah Faver. p. 32

LEWIS L. DAVIS, dec., Dec. 23, 1833. Paid heirs: Bailess R. Crosby in right of his wife; Eliza T. Daniel. Minors: Isaiah Davis, Wm. L. Davis, Andrew J. Davis, Isobella Davis, Caroline M. Davis, Nancy Davis. p. 350

CHARLES PETTUS, dec., Jan. 7, 1833. Division of negroes. Heirs: Mrs. Mariah Pettus, Sarah Pettus, "willed to them by their uncle, Garland Wingfield". p. 197

JOEL T. SMITH, Elizabeth S. Smith, exr., Sept., 1832. Division. Legatees: Micajah Biddle, Andrew Huling, George Smith, Henry B. Smith, Amelia Smith, Mariah and Margaret Smith. p. 226

ELIZABETH O. D. BOROM, dec., Inventory, Sept.18, 1833. p. 256

JOHN N. SIMPSON, dec., Jan. 5, 1831, Division of negroes: James B. Simpson, William, John, Felix G., Charles N., Thomas P. Simpson. p. 74

JOHN WALKER, dec., 1827 and 1829. Division of negroes. William Q. Anderson, in right of his wife Sophia; Robert Martha, Richard G. and James S. Walker; Joel Callaway in right of his wife Nancy; the children of William Walker, dec., to-wit: James, Meriwether and William Walker, minors, p. 110

ALLEN HOLLIDAY, dec., Division of negroes, July 25, 1848. Distributees: Jacintha R. Holliday, J. R. Holliday, A. F. Holliday, Wyche Jackson in right of his wife, Franc A. C. Holliday. Returns 1843-48, p. 277

J. B. HOLMES, dec., R. J. Willis, adm., Settlement, May 4, 1836. Distributees: B. B. Reeves, A. North, Mary Holmes, Jesse M. Hobiny. Paid R. J. Willis as gdn. Returns 1833-38, p. 401

ANNUAL RETURNS BOOK 1836-1841

JAMES LYLE, dec., John Finley, adm., April 1841. Paid heirs: John O. Hackney, Elizabeth Martha, Rebecca and James Lyle, minors. p. 255

JOHN COLEMAN, dec., John Q. West, gdn., Mch. 1837. Received cash from estate of Mrs. Sarah Coleman, dec., of Virginia. Minors: Emily, George W., Sarah T., John J., Joseph T. Coleman, p. 101-04

JESSE SLACK, dec., Thomas and John Slack, adms., Jan. 6, 1838. Division. Heirs: John Holton in right of wife Hannah; Amos W.

Todd (,), Job R. Hinton, Jesse Slack, George Slack, Thomas Slack, Jacob Slack, Jacob Hinton. Book of Returns 1836-39, p. 258

JESSE FAULKNER HEARD, dec., John Wilkinson, adm., Sept. 3, 1836. Accts. Tuition for Wm. T. Heard, Caroline W., Eliza J., Stephen, Faulkner, Ann W., Benj. W., and Henrietta Heard. p. 125

WILLIAM SIMPSON, dec., Francis C. Armstrong, adm. Mch. 2, 1840. Paid heirs: Catherine and Elizabeth Simpson, Mary Wingfield, David Simpson. Tuition for C. and E. Simpson, p. 170

ISAAC WHITTAKER, dec., Enoch Callaway, adm. Returns for year 1838. Paid James M. Whitaker, Harden P. Whitaker, p. 109

MRS. PELOT, of Abbeville, S. C., dec., John F. Pelot, adm. Mrs. Frances F. Pelot, gdn. of Francis L. Pelot, son of decendent. June 15, 1839, p. 276

JOHN ROBERTSON, dec., May 21, 1836. Paid legatees: Ann Robertson, Maria Robertson, Sarah Robertson, William Rutledge in right of his wife. p. 51

SAMUEL M. SMITH, dec., Settlement. Nov. 11, 1836. Paid James M. Smith, Albert H. Shipherd, George M. Smith, Mary H. Smith. Returns 1836-1841, p. 59, 135

FRANCIS BUTLER, dec., Division, Jan. 1838. Distributees: Elizabeth E. Willis, Frances A. Butler, David E. Butler, p. 167

GARRATT NEWMAN, dec., Nemartha Newman, adm. Division 1849. H eirs: N. Newman, Henry J. Newman, D. A. Newman, Richard Newman, Thomas Newman, Permelia Frazer, husband, James M. Frazer. Original record, box file, Newman family. See allso Appr., Sales and Distributions 1848-53, p. 154

JOHN B. LEONARD, dec., Jan. 4, 1837. Devisees: Mrs. Mary Leonard, Ludwell M. Leonard, Wm. P. Leonard, John B. Peonard, Edward and Thomas Leonard, Royland Beasley, John B. Greene, William H. Dyson. Book of Invt., Sales and Divisions. Returns 1836-1841, pp. 131-136

JANE JACKSON, dec. A. S. Jackson, adm. Paid heirs: J. B. Jackson, Sarah Jackson, Johnson W. Jackson, William D. Jackson, Mercer and John H. Jackson. Returns 1836-1841, p. 110

WILLIAM NORMAN, dec. John H. Norman, adm. June 15, 1841. Settlement with heirs: Johnson Norman, Johnson Norman as gdn. of Henry W. Norman, Felix Norman, Henry Spratlin for Irvin Jackson. Equal shares. Returns 1836-41, p. 271

JAMES WRIGHT, dec. James H. Flynt, gdn. Settlement; John M. Wright; B. Proctor; his share of land in Troupe Co.; Wm. C. Wright Mch. 2, 1840. Returns 1836-1841, p. 174. William C. and John M. Wright, minors in 1838. Same book, p. 143

JOURNAL YY - RETURNS

JOHN FINLEY, dec. Division 1859. Distributees: Mrs. Gracey Rounceville; Mrs. Elizabeth Lyle; the children of David Lyle; Thomas Greene; Mrs. Sappington's children; James T. Finley. "six shares. Eleven distributees". p. 500

DR. R. S. CALLAWAY, dec. Division in part Dec. 10, 1857. James V. Drake in right of his wife, Sarah A. L. Callaway. Other children, minors, not given in this record YY p. 450. Seaborn Callaway, adm. May 2, 1853. Admrs. Bond Book 1849-1876, p. 240

H. L. EMBRY, dec. Division in part. Paid Sarah Jane Lovelace, formerly Embry. Dec. 1853, Journal YY, p. 70

H. L. EMBRY, dec. Divsion, Dec. 1858. Paid John J. Embry and James D. McCreary, Journal YY, p. 463

JESSE WILLIAMS, dec. E. R. Anderson, adm. Division Dec. 24, 1853. Heirs: Mary Muse, wife of Wm. P. Muse, George M. Williams, son of Jesse, dec., Martha M. Terrell, wife of Booker Terrell; Joseph M. Williams; Jesse C. Williams; Nancy Ann Blakey; wife of Benjamine Blakey, William M. Blakey, Sarah J. Williams. Journal YY, p. 74

ENOCH CALLAWAY, dec. Paid distributees: Thomas N. Rhodes, S. Callaway, F. M. Cheney, James F. Geer, William O. Cheney; Brantley M. Callaway, A. B. Callaway, Christopher Binns, James H. Spratlin, Aris R. Callaway, and Reuben Callaway's children: Virginia J., Chandler M., and Reuben H. Callaway, minors. Dec. 12, 1859, p. 530

FELIX HENDERSON, dec. John H. Dyson, adm. Dec. 29, 1858. Division. Heirs: Mrs. Emma Williams, formerly E. Henderson; Joseph W. Henderson, and five minors. p. 464

JOHN HUGULEY, dec. Division. Dec. 1853. Heirs: George Huguley, Susannah, Amos, Mahala, James Sullivan, Thomas Huguley, John Huguley, Job Huguley, Ransome Huguley. p. 66

JAMES NOLAN, dec. John West and James W. Nolan, exrs. Devisees: Nancy West, Frances A. Huguley, Polly Bolton, daughters: James W.

John West

Nolan, Thomas F. Nolan, John H. Nolan, sons. p. 339. Refer to next probate book #10

JOHN R. PETEET, dec. Dec. 30, 1857. Division: Milton R. Barrett in right of his wife Sarah; John J. Peteet; Mary J. Peteet; Susan Peteet. p. 437

JAMES C. TALBOT, dec. Sarah Talbot, gdn. Division. Dec. 28, 1953. Sarah E. Colley, George T. Talbot, E. J. Talbot, M. H. Talbot, H. A. Talbot. p. 32

THOMAS TALBOT, dec. Elihu Talbot, adm. Division of negroes Nov.1853. Distributees: Henry A. Jones, representative of Mary Mosely, dau. of Thomas Talbot, dec.; Dr. L. C. Belt, representing Elizabeth Creswell Jones, dau. of decendent; Matthew Talbot, son of decendent; Sarah A. Talbot, widow of the late James C. Talbot, son of said Thomas, dec.; Elihu Talbot, son of said Thomas, dec. YY pages 17 to 28. Inventory same book, p. 9

MATTHEW TALBOT, dec. Nov. 21, 1855. F. F.Simpson, adm. Distributees: The heirs of James C. Talbot: Sarah E. Colley, George Talbot, F. F. Simpson, Matthew Talbot, Harriett Talbot. Journal YY, p. 247

MATTHEW TALBOT, dec. Nov. 1855, Division. Distributees: Elihu Talbot; Dr. L. C. Belt; Heirs of James C. Talbot. Journal YY, p. 246 (Inventory and Sale, same booke, pages 221-229)

ANNUAL RETURNS BOOK NO. 10

MATTHEW TALBOT, dec. F. F. Simpson, adm. Oct. 22, 1857, Paid. Distribution of Estates - 1816-1856 - Page 9

Elihu Talbot, paid L. C. Belt, each $1,743. Paid George Talbot, S. E. Talbot, M. H. Talbot, H. A. Talbot (by G. T. Talbot) $348, each. The last four, evidently, are grandchildren. p. 387

WILLIAM JEFFRIES, dec., James T. Hackney, adm. Feb. 1854. "Nancy Jeffries moved to Chambers Co., Ala." Returns #10, p. 164. Returns, same book p. 347. Paid Catherine Hackney, Dorothy Wall, Howell, Harrison, Sara A. Lindsey, Nancy Jeffries.

JAMES NOLAN, dec. John West, exr. Returns Apr. 5, 1856. John & Thomas Nolan, minors. John W. Nolan, Polly Bolton's children, Wm. H. Huguley, John W. Bolton, John West's wife's share. Expense of going to and from Texas mentioned. Expense to Calhoun Co., to Stewart Co. to sell land. Executor states his wife

John West

had special legacy. Returns No. 11, "John Nolan died in West Baton Rouge Parish, La." while traveling to Wharton, Texas. P. 37

FELIX M. HENDERSON, dec. John H. Dyson, gdn. of minors: Felix M., Thomas A., Joseph W., Emma H., Sarah M. Henderson. Returns No. 10, p. 83

JOHN WILKINSON, dec., Samuel W. Wynn, exr. John D. Cooper, gdn. of minors: Ann T. Wilkinson; E. A. Wilkinson; paid John A. Heard his share; paid Floride V. Wilkinson. Returns No. 10, p. 49. Remark: Bible records show other children.

JOHN S. WALTON, dec., I. T. Irvin, Jr. gdn. of minors: Isabella, J. S., and Wm. S. Walton, 1854. Expenses traveling to Tennessee. Returns No. 10, p. 277

JOHN PERTEET, dec. W. R. Perteet, adm. Paid heirs: Minors of John R. Perteet; William Maxwell; William P. Watkins; B. Appling, and wife, Elizabeth D. Johns. Feb. 17, 1857. Returns No. 10, p.346

JOHN R. PETEET, dec. James H. Lane, gdn. of minors: Sarah E., Mary J., Susan E., John R. Peteet, for year 1853. Returns No. 10, p.144

H. L. EMBRY, dec., Thomas Dyer, exr. James D. McBreary, gdn. of minors: Cinthia D. Little, formerly Embry; Mrs. S. J. Embry; Eliza J. Embry; James S. Embry; H. L. Embry; Emily Embry; John Embry. Accts. for 1852. Returns No. 10, p. 52

ELIZA BALL, dec., Lewis S. Brown, adm. Aug. 1853. Paid Heirs: Simpson Fouche, Alexander Pope, Garnett Andrews, D. S. Ball, Fred Ball, equal shares. Returns No. 10, p. 88

T. L. WOOTTEN, dec., Henry P. Wootten, gdn. of minors: J. L.; J. F.; H. W.; Mary P.; Thomas W.; Sarah A.; and C. T. Wootten. Returns No. 10, p. 66.

C. H. WOOTTEN, dec., Henry P. Wootten, gdn. Minors Accts: Mch. 1853 Caroline, Mary E. and H. P. Wootten. p. 63

JAMES HINTON, dec., Henry P. Wootten, exr. Mch. 31, 1853. Devisees: Jesse Hinton paid in full; B. B. Hinton in full; William L. Wootten in full; James W. Hinton in full; William H. Peters in full; by William D. Quinn, agt. Returns No. 10, p. 59

ELIZABETH THOMAS, dec., James Marks, Esq., adm. Paid heirs: W. H. Crain in full; John H. Marks, Sr. in full; Joel E. Crain. The Crain heirs, viz: Eleanor Crane, Burton Crane, Warren Crane. L. N. Pinkard, gdn. Thomas Pinkard, also Nicholas Thompkins, by his atty. Irby H. Scott. John P. Henry and Catherine Henry. Wm. H. Marks, Wm. Coats, James M. Hawkins, trustee. O. H. Kenan, Mary Cargile; James H. Pinkard, also heirs of Jno. Tompkins: James B. Marks and W. M. Marks and N. M. Marks; also James Pinkard, Martha Williams. Nov. 1852. Returns No. 10, p. 85. Mention of sale of land in Cobb Co., Ga. Elizabeth calls all legatees her nieces and nephews. The case was settled in Chancery Court. Returns No. 10,p.85

W. HANSON, dec., W. M. Hanson, adm. Aug. 26, 1856. Paid heirs: Mary E. Hanson, John M. Hanson; M. S. Hanson, gdn. for Henry Hanson; also the "minors of F. H. Adams"; Haley Fortson, Margaret A. Hanson, and Margaret S. Hanson. Returns No. 10, p. 315

CATHERINE E. HANSON, W. M. Hanson, adm. Aug. 26, 1856. Paid heirs: Wm. S. Hanson, gdn. of Henry Hanson, minor; also for minors of F. H. Adams (2), Mary E. Hanson (3), John M. Hanson (4), Margaret A. Hanson (5), Haley Fortson (6), Margaret S. Hanson (7), Returns No. 10, p. 315. Remark: The record shows Mary E., John M., Henry Hanson were minors of F. H. Adams

JAMES L. CALLAWAY, dec., and Tabitha Callaway, dec. John Callaway gdn. of minors. Distribution: James Callaway, minor, to receive one half of estate; the other half to be divided among Tabitha Callaway (one third part to her) and the balance equally divided among the minors of Wm. Thurmond, dec. Date 1837. Ref. Returns 1836-1839, p. 202. Returns 1836 to 1841, p. 145

THOMAS FAVER, dec., W. D. Walton, L. D. Faver , adms. Dec. 14, 1861. Settlement with heirs: N. H. Faver, W. T. Howard, L. D. Faver, W. D. Walton, D. Walton, W. W. Faver, James D. Faver. Returns No. 11, p. 117

HOWARD FAVER, dec. W. D. Walton, L. D. Faver, adm. Division, Oct. 27, 1859. Mrs. Nancy H. Faver, William W. Faver, James Faver, Wm. D. Walton, Daniel Walker, Wm. T. Howard, distributees. Journal YY, p. 491

WM. THURMOND, dec., Henry Pope adm., 1837. Mary & Nancy Thurmond, minors. Returns Bk. 1836-1841, p. 180

WM. THURMOND, dec., Division of negroes, Jan. 6, 1836. James L. Callaway in right of his wife, Tabitha; Mary Catherine Thurmond; Nancy Pope Thurmond. Returns 1830-1836, p. 460

ANNUAL RETURNS BY ADMINISTRATORS AND GUARDIANS

1833 - - - - - - 1838

WILKES COUNTY - Ordinary's Office
Inferior Court
Distribution of Estates

JOHN C. POPE, dec., John T. Wootten, adm., Jan. 8, 1835. Division among heirs: Wylie H. Pope, James Huling, Mary Pope Bradford; Wylie M. Pope, Mary Pope. p. 286

JOHN M. WEST, dec., William West, adm. Paid Ann C. West on estate of Eleanor Nelson. Paid John West his share on est. E. Nelson, and as adm. of Stephen Harris, dec., two shares. Paid Mary S. West on est. E. Nelson. Paid John Thornton his share of E. Nelson est. Paid Ann C. West her share of E. Nelson est. Paid Seymore Catchings his legacy, est. E. Nelson. Paid Mary Ann West her share of E. Nelson est., Jan. 3, 1837, p. 448. Same book p. 264 John M. West, dec., Wm. West gdn. of Charles Pinkney West, received his share, Apr. 6, 1835. John Thornton, gdn. of Nancy C. West, received her share, p. 108. The same children of John M. West, dec., received payment of their deceased father's estate, 1838, p. 109

MARY GRANT, dec., Robert Toombs, adm., Apr. 22, 1836. Paid legatees: James Griffin, Amelia A. Grant, "et al", p. 352

JOHN SHEARMAN, dec., Jan. 2, 1835. Division: Owen S. Shearman; Thomas Shearman; Johh J., orphan of John Shearman, dec.; James Shearman. Jan. 2, 1835, p. 306

ARCHIBALD RIDDLE, dec., Sarah Y. Riddle, gdn. of minors: Thomas, Archibald, Anderson, Asher, and Watkins Riddle. Apr. 17, 1835, p.282

THOMAS HEMPHILL, dec., Aaron A. Cleveland, adm. Feb. 26, 1833. Distributees: Emily and Cyrus Hemphill, minors. Paid jointly. P. 86

CATHERINE HENDRICKS, dec., Nancy McRea, adm. Apr. 3, 1835. Paid heirs: David and Catharine Aughtry; Mary E. and B. B. Russell; Nancy E. Dismukes, paid in part. Cash paid M. Lane as gdn. of Mary E. and B. B. Russell, 1835, p. 254.

THOMAS FORMBY, dec., Larkin Formby, adm. July 21, 1824. Settlement with heirs: Robert T. Dawson, Henry T. Dawson, Abraham Whitaker; Nolan Formby, Nancy and Richard Formby, Charles McKnight, p. 216

NANCY M. MONTGOMERY, dec., David Montgomery, adm. Heirs: John G. Colbert, N. W. Smith, Joseph White, W. E. Robertson, Mary Montgomery, Susan White, David Montgomery. Nov. 4, 1834, p. 270

JOHN FANNING, dec., Reuben Faver, gdn. Nov. 1832. Paid minors or gdn.: Bryan Fanning, Malcome Fanning; Patsy, wife of John Wise; William Matthews, and Reuben Faver, p. 49

WILLIAM B. WILLIS, dec., Daniel Owen, adm. Paid Wm. C. Neel, who married Mary P. Willis. May 1834, p. 146

REUBEN DOGGETT, dec., Benjamine Paul gdn. Accts: Mary Doggett, Mariah M. Doggett minors, for year 1831, p. 45

JOSEPH A. HEWELL, dec., Booker Lipscomb, gdn. July 6, 1835. Accts. of minors John and Joseph H ewell, p. 311

JOHN HEARD, dec. Wm. Q. Anderson, adm. Paid James L., John, Elizabeth, Thomas S., John A., and Thomas A. Heard. Mch. 3, 1834, p. 192

JOHN EDWARDS, dec., William Worrell, adm. Sept. 5, 1836. Settlement with heirs: Sampson Brown, Henry Jackson, Jesse Bradshaw, Henry Bradshaw, p. 414

SIMPSON H. WILLIAMS, dec., David Hillhous and Harrison Williams, adms. Jan. 6, 1834. Heir receipts: Thomas Williams; John Pickin; Hanson Dove, in right of his mother; Elias Williams; Peter Davis; Harrison Williams, who mentions he is son of decedent . p. 76

WILLIAM A. GRANT, dec., and MARY GRANT, dec. Joseph W. Robinson, adm. Division of negroes Jan. 3, 1835. Mrs. Eugenia Griffin, Amelia A. Grant, Robert A. Toombs, as adm. of Mrs. Mary Grant, dec., three equal shares, p. 290

JAMES CREWS, dec. R. J. Willis, adm. Mch. 10, 1835. Settlement with heirs: Stephen W. Barkswell, husband of Susan Crews; S. W. Willis, Thomas N. Heard, husband of Emily Crews; L. H. Willis, husband of Nancy Crews, and Benedictine Crews. Remark: Benedictine was widow of decedent, p. 273

THOMAS WINGFIELD, dec. John W. Butler, adm. May 21, 1836. Paid equal share: heirs, William Reed, Peter B. Terrell, Wm. A. Terrell, John E. Robinson, p. 401

LEWIS L. DAVIS, dec., Isaiah T. Irvin, adm. Feb. 6, 1834. Paid Bailor Crosby, Nancy Davis, Caroline Davis, "et al", p. 164

THOMAS EIDSON, dec., Philip Combs, adm. Nov. 4, 1833. Paid Shares: Lucy Cosby's children: Alfred G. Perry, who married Sallie Eidson., p. 130

EDWARD ECHOLS, dec., Van Allen Echols, adm. Feb. 4, 1831, will annexed. Paid Alfred Carowth, distributee, by will of Nathan Echols, dec. p. 120-22

THOMAS EIDSON, dec., Philip Combs, adm. May 1831. Paid Lesley Coats' children their distributive share. Thos. R. Eidson, gdn., p. 116

FRANCIS GIDDENS, dec., Elizabeth Giddens, adm., May 10, 1834. Receipts by heirs: Taliaferro Jones (land in Jackson Co.) Edward Giddens, James K. Giddens, p. 289

ISAAC CALLAWAY, dec., Jno. P. Barrett and Mary Callaway, exrs. Sept. 4, 1837 Paid John H. Low his part of the estate, p. 489

ELIZABETH WINGFIELD, dec., John M. Butler, gdn. Mary L. Wingfield, now Robinson a minor, Apr. 2, 1835, p. 250

SAMUEL M. SMITH, dec., James M. Smith, adm., Dec. 23, 1836. Paid Geo. M. Smith, Wm. H. Smith, A. H. Shepherd and S. H. Shepherd, distributees. James M. Smith, gdn. of Geo. M. Smith, and Wm. H. Smith, p. 479. Two records - additional information.

ANNUAL RETURNS 1828 - 1831

JOSEPH BURKS, dec. Fortune Burks, adm. Jan. 28. Division. Distributees: Fortune Burks, widow of Dec; Joseph H. Burks; Benajah S. Burks; William Burks; Willis Fullilove, in right of his wife, Clary, Hudson Burke; Frances, Mary and John Slack, children of Benjamine Slack; William McLendon in right of his wife Betsy; John Burks; Luke Barton, in right of his wife Lucy; Daniel C. Heard, in right of his wife Nancy; Charles Burks; Wylie P. Burks. Jan. 28, 1828, p. 199

EDWARD LYON, dec., Elizabeth Lyon, adm. Estate divided. Heirs not named. Dec. 17, 1833

PHILIP COMBS, dec., Feb. 1, 1847. Sale of negroes. Buying at sale: Mrs. Elizabeth Combs, Jeremiah R. Combs, Mrs. Sarah Marlow, Miss Nancy Combs, Philip F. Combs, John Staples, Edward Waller. Returns 1843-1848, p. 242. (Some returns on this Revolutionary soldier's estate lost. Deeds of gift available.

JOHN HEARD, dec. Division May, 1843. Mark and Charles Heard, minors, of John Heard, dec. Return Book 1843-48, p. 116

JOSEPH BEALLE, dec., Mary H. Bealle, adm. Mch. 1842. Distributees: Mary Bealle, Mary H. Bealle, Wm. M. Beall, Joseph H. and John A. Beall, Patrick J. Barnett, Albert A. Beall. Returns 1839-1844, p. 233

SAMUEL WINGFIELD, dec., Charles Wingfield, adm. Division of negroes: Francis Wingfield, Mrs. Wingfield, William C. Wingfield, Archibald S. Wingfield, distributees. Dec. 26, 1821. Returns Book 1821-25, p. 67

JOSEPH HENDERSON, dec. Division Feb. 9, 1842. H. Thompson for his children: Jesse M. Henderson; Felix G. Henderson; Jacob Lyons, Leving? Henderson; Thompson Malone. Returns Book, 1839-44, p.250

ABNER WELLBORN, dec. Division of negroes. Mrs. Martha Wellborn; Miss Ann Wellborn; Abner R. Wellborn; Miss Martha Wellborn; dau. Hepsiba Wellborn; Dr. A. B. Calhoun; Wilkes R. Wellborn, co-heirs. Returns 1839-1844, p.

JOHN COLEMAN, dec., Joseph T. Coleman, dec., a minor. John Q. West, gdn. Division. Dec. 3, 1844. Chenoth Callaway and Elish H. Daniel, legatees.

JOHN COLEMAN, dec., John Q. West, gdn. of minors. Heirs and distributees, in right of their father, John Coleman, dec. (from Thompson Coleman grandfather, dec.) James D. Gresham, who married Sarah F. Coleman, minor of said John, dec.; Richard Leonard his share, Emily A.; Joseph T.; George W.; Thomas L.; John L. Coleman. Paid minors, 1839. Returns 1836-41, p. 278

IGNATIUS DODSON, dec., Charles Dodson, adm., Chloe Ann Dodson, dec. widow of Ignatius. Division Jan. 4, 1825. Distributees: Catherine Dodson, Thomas Ignatius Dodson, Charles Terrell, Chloe Ann Dodson, minor. Geo. W. Doson, Wm. A. Terrell, Charles Dodson, Mariah Dodson. Book of Appr. and Returns 1824 to 1828, p. 34, also p. 12. Chloe Ann Dodson married Stephen Arnold, May 26, 1825.

ZIMRI A. TATE, dec., Enos Tate, adm. Distribution, Jan. 1844. Mrs. Sarah Tate, now Mrs. Sarah Wingfield. Second division: Archibald S. Wingfield in right of his wife, Sarah Wingfield, widow of said Zimri. Enos A. Tate, minor of the heirs. Returns 1839-44, p. 327

ROBERT TOOMBS, dec., Henry J. Pope, gdn. of minors. Heirs: Robert A. Toombs, James H. Toombs, Catherine Toombs, Sarah Ann Tombs, Gabriel Toombs, and L. C. Toombs, dec. Date 1831. Book of Annual Returns, 1833-1838, p. 63.
A full acct. of this estate is found in Early Ga. Records, Vol. 2, p. 302. (Davidson)

WILKES COUNTY

WILLS
1830 -- 1860

Wills recorded in Wilkes County Book "11" (eleven in the Office of Judge of Inferior Court, now Ordinary's Office. Wills of later dates recorded in this Book are not included herein.

Page 50 ALLISON, REBECCA, Jan. 30, 1841. May term 1841. To Presbyterian Minister. To Gainham Rakestraw for self and for Mary E. Blair and her children, in trust for Nancy E. Pomroy, to go to Josephine A. Aughtry, and Wm. H. Aughtry, the children of Catharine Aughtry. Mentions Benj. Russell. To the children of my deceased brother James McRae of Virginia, six tracts of land in Kentucky. Exrs: Mark A. Lane, Garland L. Rakestraw. Wit: Royland Beasley, Simeon Hester, Lewis Brown.

ANDERSON, THOMAS, Oct. 8, 1857; Feb. 4, 1860. To wife certain property in trust of Exrs. Son John R. Anderson has received his part. To Edmund Anderson's children one equal share in trust of Exrs. Balance of estate to be divided equally among my daughters: Mrs. Render, Mrs. Willis, Mrs. Barksdale, Mrs. Walton, Mrs. Webster, Mrs. Leslie and Wm. Q. Anderson. Exrs: Wm. Q. Anderson with James D. Willis. Codicil: Wm. Q. Anderson having departed this life, Thomas W. Callaway with James D. Willis appt. exrs. Oct. 4, 1859. Wit: Wm. Dyson, Garnett Andrews, Nicholas Wylie. Codicil: Oct. 8, 1859. To my gr. sons Andrew and James Anderson, sons of my deceased son John R. Anderson, April 5, 1860. p. 308

Page 215 ANTHONY, ANN. July 7, 1852; Sept. 1854. To William Q. Anderson in trust for Lucinda Lane, wife of Micajah Lane, the land including my brick house, all furniture and all adjacent property. To Alex. Pope, Sr., to friend Dr. James H. Lane. To Bolling Anthony Pope. To Ann Anthony Pope, and her brothers and sisters. To Eliza Lane. To niece Lucy Gordon and her husband, David Gordon. To David E. Butler and to Rev. V. R. Thornton, foreign mission property. To Judith B lakey, widow of Thomas B lakey. For Wm. Q. Anderson in trust for dau. Nancy Anthony, wife of Matthew Anthony. Makes provision for grave stones for each of the family. To my brother Osborn Stone, that part coming to Anderson and William Stone, sons of my brother, Osborn Stone. To brother Osborn Stone and to his other children. To the children of my sister Elizabeth Cain, that part coming to Elizabeth Sherrer, and Elizabeth Miller in right of their Mother. To David Gordon of Alabama. Exrs: Wm. Q. Anderson, Edward R. Anderson, Alex. Pope, Jr. - - - -? Vickers.

Page 267 ANTHONY, MARY R. Sept. 20, 1859; Jan. 1860. To youngest children Edwin, Willie, James and Julia Anthony. To eldest children: E. Dubose Anthony, Mary Louisa Jones. Emma Hill, Isabella Stokes. Exrs: James R. DuBose. Robert Toombs. Wit: G. Toombs, R. H. Vickers, Wm. M. Reese.

Page 101 ANTHONY, MICAJAH T. Feb. 2, 1836; Sept. 13, 1843. To Wife Mary R. Anthony my whole estate. Wife Sole exr. Wit: Chenowith Callaway, Robert Toombs, Wm. M. Reese.

Page 60 APPLING, JOEL. July 17, 1833; July 6, 1841. To wife Mary. To sons Joel, Lewis, John, Burwell and Harman Appling. To children of my dec. Daus. Sarah Baker and Susan Favor. To the five children of my son Thomas Applihg, one eleventh part of my estate. To children of my decd. daus. Sarah Baker and Susan Favor when all of their children are of age. To sons Samuel Lewis and Harman Appling, one eleventh part to each. To the rest of my children now living, three equal shares. Mentions Mary Spratlin. Exrs: Wife Mary, John and Burwell Appling. Wit: John H. Norman, Jesse Spratlin.

Page 228 ARMER, AMANDA E. Dec. 29, 1854; Feb. 7, 1855. Formerly Amanda E. Norman. To son Thomas Bolton Armer. To my children by my first husband: Isaac, William, Norman, Rachael, Elizabeth and Felix Ann Norman. Exrs: Uncle, Dr. Geo. W. Bolton. Wit: Geo. L. Norman, L. M. Hill.

Page 14 ARMSTRONG, JAMES, M. G. Aug. 1807; Sept. 4, 1837. To my wife Elizabeth, all estate except my library which I lend to Mercer Institute, to be given to the first of my sons that may be called to the Ministry. I appoint wife Elizabeth exrs., she to make such disposition among the children as she wishes. The remaining property to be divided according to a contract by her, recorded in Clerk's Office in Savannah, Ga. Wit: Chas. L. Bolton, Nicholas Wylie. Remark. Such contacts usually found in Deed Books.

Page 331 ARNOLD, ALLEN J. Sept. 5, 1860; Apr. Court 1863. To wife Eunice Arnold, large amount of property to her and her children. Balance of estate to be divided among my children: Simeon C., Moses H., Oliver H. P. Arnold, Susan D. McKenney (or McKemsey), Richard P. Arnold, minor. And to son-in-law Cicero McKenney in trust for son R. P. Arnold. Exr: Moses Arnold and Cicero McKemsey.

Page 380 BAILEY, GEORGE. July 24, 1866; Sept. 3, 1866. To dau. Mary Harris all estate at wife's death to become the property of my gr. children: Mary G., Sarah E., James W. H., Eugenia C. W., and Victoria J.C. Patterson. Son George S., and dau. Delilah Bailey to have joint interest. Mentions deceased son, John H. Bayley. Exrs: Son George S. and my dau. Mary. Wit: J. M. Dyson, Henry T. Harper, G. G. Norman.

Page 281 BAILEY, RUSSELL. Feb. 19, 1849; Oct. 2, 1860. To my children by wife Betsey Bailey: Russell, Simon, John, Gracey, Sarah Ann Bailey. To Car Bailey and to my children by Peggy Bailey. Exrs: John Dyson, son George Bailey. Wit: J. B. Sanders, Lewis S. Brown.

Page 103 BAIRD, WILLIAM. Feb. 2, 1836; Sept. 10, 1839. To wife my plantation; at her death to son William. To daus. Amy Bradley, Barsheba Bradford, Serena R. Baird, and Catharine Baird. To orphens of my deceased son James, in trust. To the children of my son Benjamine. Exrs: Wm. D. Bradley, Richard Bradford, Wm. R. Baird, Benjamine Baird. Wit: Augustine D. Statham, Wm. Jackson.

Page 108 BANKSTON, LAWRENCE. Apr. 10, 1834; Nov. 22, 1844. To wife Nancy the land I live on, and numerous gifts, which are to be divided among my four daus; Isabella Irvin, Priscilla Matthews, Elizabeth Mosely (?), Martha Sappington. To son Isaac Whittaker. To gr. dau. Sarah Truitt, wife of John Truitt. To gr. son Alfred Shorter. The rest of estate to four daus. named above, and to the heirs of Hyrom Bankston, dec. with exception that gr. son Weldon L. Bankston draw one half of distributive share coming to said orphans, and the other half to the other children of Hyrom Bankston, dec'd. Exrs: Son-in-law. Isaiah T. Irvin, Caleb Sappington, Wit: W. Johnson, Daniel Woolbright, Wm. Sherrer.

Page 245 BARNETT, ELIZA W. Nov. 22, 1849; July 7, 1856. To daus. Emma M. and Mary L. Barnett. Exrs: Daughters. Wit: Lewis S. Brown, Stephen G. Pettus, A. J. Massengale.

Page 82 BARNETT, SAMUEL. Dec. 15, 1842; Mch. 4, 1843. To son-in-law Alexander Pope. To son-in-law Archibald S. Wingfield. To wife Elizabeth Barnett. Sons Samuel J., and Augustus Barnett to receive Collegiate course; My two daus. Emma and Mary L. Barnett to continue at the Washington Female Seminary. Exrs: Wife and Francis Willis. Wit: E. M. Burton, Thomas Semmes. Codicil: By will of John Joyner, dec. in S. Carolina, I am entitled to certain property; I give my share to children of my dau. Sarah Joyner Pope and to children of my dau. Sarah Ann Wingfield. Signed Jan. 5, 1843.

Page 209 BELL, JOHN. Feb. 2, 1851; Feb. 6, 1854. To wife Polly Ann and to "all my children". Exr. John R. Semmes. Wit: J. R. Snead, Lucius Gartrell, James Wingfield.

Page 224 BENSON, WM. Nov. 10, 1854; Nov. 20, 1854. To my sister, Sarah Benson. To brother Joseph A. Benson and his children: Josephine, Pierce, Lumpkin, Martha, Jane, America, Sarah Elizabeth Benson.
Exrs: John N. Chenault, James Barksdale. Wit: Thomas V. Lowe, E. W. Roberts, John G. Collins.

Page 1 BLAKEY, CHURCHILL. Oct. 2, 1829; Jan. 24, 1837. To sons: Reuben, Bolling, Churchill Blakey, Jr. To son James Blakey, the land I live on. To daus: Mary Anderson, Catherine Blakey. Penelope J. Wootten. To gr. dau. Ann Roberts. To gr. son George Blakey Smith. Exrs: James Blakey, Thomas Wootten. Wit: Moses Sutton, Thomas Blakey, Churchill Blakey, Jr.

Page 343 BLAKEY, C. JUDITH. Nov. 28, 1859; Apr. 10, 1866. Of advanced age. To my son Joseph T. Blakey one sixth of my estate. To dau. Amanda H. C. Sutton and her son Reuben Saffold, one sixth. To son Benjamine C. Blakey, one sixth. To son Bolling A. Blakey one sixth. To son Churchill Blakey one sixth. To children of son Mark A. Blakey, one sixth. Exrs: Bolling A. and Benjamine C. Blakey. Wit: Wm. R. Smith, George W. Williams, Dudley Jones.

Page 210 BOOKER, RICHARDSON. Nov. 18, 1853; Nov. 21, 1853. To wife Easter Booker, property, according to a deed of gift Sept. 17, 1851. To son Efford M. Booker land he lived on, 700 acres, and negroes. To son Simpson Booker, negroes. To son Jabez M. Booker, negroes and plantation on which he lives. To gr. daus. Martha Booker and Elizabeth Booker, Nancy Booker, negroes. To sons, Leroy Booker, John M. Booker, land, etc. To Thomas J. Booker negroes and plantation on which he lives, to belong to his children. To two gr. children, youngest children of Wm. M. Booker, cash for education. Careful provision is made for slaves; families not to be separated. My son James S. Booker to be well supported. Old slaves to remain with my wife; after her death, slaves to choose whom they prefer to serve. To daus. America McGehee and Elizabeth Kendrick negroes and cash. Other negroes to be divided among my children and gr. children, they to choose masters. Exrs: Wife and Efford M. Booker. Wit: James J. Harper, Matthew McCorkle, G. G. Norman. Codicil: In which he gives legacy to gr. children, Efford and Mary Booker, children of Wm. M. Booker. Additional gifts to sons and daus. Date, Jan. 6, 1854.

Page 259 BOOKER, RICHARDSON. Deed of gift to wife Easter Booker, negroes Dafney, old Soloman, old Nancy, old Pegg and her ten children, Harriet and her five children, also gr. children of old Peggy and many other negroes named in the deed, including old Caesar, husband of old Peggy. Sept. 17, 1851. Test: Timothy Duffee, Horace E. Paschal, Thos. H. Wootten. Proved before grand jury. Recorded June 7, 1859.

Page 15 BOOKER, WILLIAM, Sr. Dec. 15, 1826; Nov. 6, 1837. To son Richardson Booker, Esq. Valuable property. To Mrs. Hester Booker, wife of my son Richardson. Exr: Son Richardson Booker. Wit: Christopher Brooks, Jno. G. Griffin, Ann Rakestraw.

Page 168 BRADLEY, WILLIAM D. Aug. 14, 1848; Nov. 6, 1848. To Lucy W. Jones. To Wm. B. Smith. To Benj. F. Bradley. To son Wm. D. Bradley. Exrs: Wife, son Wm. D. Bradley. Wit: Wm. Jackson, Richard Bradford, Wm. Quinn.

Page 238 BRADLEY, W. D. Oct. 5, 1855; Nov. 28, 1855. To Mother-in-law, Mrs. Mary McLendon. To wife Clary. To all my children. Exrs: Brother Benjamine F. Bradley, Taliaferro Jones. Wit: W. D. Quinn, F. M. Stribling.

Page 146 BRANHAM, FRANCIS. Nov. 17, 1840; Sept. 28, 1846. To Brother Henry

Terrell, in trust for my dau. Mary W. Branham. To son John T. Branham. To dau. Sarah E. Branham. To dau. Frances Walker. Exr: Brother Henry Terrell. Wit: John H. Pope. John Pettus, A. S. Wingfield.

Page 278 BROWN, LEWIS S. June 11, 1858; June 1858. To wife Sarah A. Brown. To sister Mrs. Ann Morgan. To Luke J. Morgan and to his son Asa S. Morgan of Arkansas. Mentions law office and library. Exr: Wife and Garnett Andrews. Wit: R. H. Vickers, Jas. E. (Waddy?), Rufus L. Forman.

Page 374 BROWN, SARAH A. Feb. 27, 1861; July 19, 1866. Late Husband; Lewis S. Brown. To Niece Anulett Andrews, wife of Judge Garnett Andrews, my house and lot. To sister, Caroline E. Willie. To niece, Sarah Pope, wife of Alexander Pope of H arrison Co. Texas. To niece Louisa Pope, dau. of Alex. Pope of Texas. To nephew James W. Pope, son of Alex. Pope. To nephews: John H. Pope, William L. Pope, Samuel B. Pope, Alexander and Asa W. Pope, children of Alex. Pope of Texas. To nephews Asa H. and James Willie of Texas. To nephew Wm. Thomas Willie of Texas. To nephew Wm. Willie of Texas. To nieces, Donomia Carter, Sarah Farley, Victoria Hoxey and Bell Shelman. To Miss Annie Morgan; if not living, her share to go to Sarah Brown of Wisconsin. To my niece Sarah Brown Fouche of Floyd Co. Ga. To John F. Andrews, Cora Butler, Henry F. Andrews, Garnett Andrews, Jr., Fannie Andrews, Metta Andrews, Marshall Andrews, the children of Garnett Andrews, Sr. To Sally Vickers, dau. of Robert H. Vickers. Gifts to Methodist Church. Gift to Henry F. Andrews and to Dr. Henry F. Andrews. Exrs: Garnett Andrews. Wit: R. H. Vickers, R. L. Foreman, S. R. Palmer.

Page 357 BURNS, SAMUEL T. Sept. 3, 1856; June 6, 1864. To wife and to three children, Samuel T., Martha E., Susannah Burns. To my two children William Burns and Adelia E. Smith one share of James Burns estate. Exr: Wm. M. Reese. Wit: A. Pope, Robert S. Smith, Wm. M. Booker.

Page 283 CADE, JAMES. Dec. 24, 1857; Dec. 24, 1857. All property to nephew Nicholas D. Carter. Exr: None. Wit: Thos. B. Norman, John L. Norman.

Page 302 CALLAWAY, CHENOTH. Jan. 24, 1861; June 5, 1861. My executors to keep my estate together for the benefit of the family and education of my children. As each child married, executor to give to them such portion of estate as they see fit, leaving ample support for wife, for life. Exrs: Brother Aristodes Callaway, Wm. M. Reese.

Page 311 CALLAWAY, SEABORN. Aug. 25, 1860; Sept. 9, 1861. To wife and children, not named. To son-in-law Simeon Parker Callaway. Exrs: Son Simeon Parker Callaway, son Henry E. Spratlin. Wit: Wm. M. Reese, Stephen R. Pettus.

Page 234 CALLAWAY, WOODSON, June 19, 1855; Sept. 3, 1855. To wife and children, not named. At the division, my children to account for that I have advanced to them. Exrs: Wife and son John. Wit: Daniel M. Anderson, Thomas C. Callaway.

Page 173 CARTER, REUBEN, May 5, 1849; July 2, 1849. To wife Mary Carter. To children Nicholas Drury Carter, Elizabeth Frances, Matilda Jane, Amos Madison Carter, equal shares. Exr: Wife. Wit: B. N. Fortson, James Morman, Elizabeth F. Carter.

Page 223 CHIVERS, JAMES A. June 26, 1854; Nov. 6, 1854. To Brother Thomas H. Chivers. To sister Jane Johnson. Exr: Brother Joel R. Chivers. Wit: John Quincey Adams, Zelotes Adams, Martha Adams. Remark: Thomas Holley Chivers, the genius, mentioned.

Page 355 CLEVELAND, AARON A. May 14, 1864; May 24, 1864. To my five daus: Ellen R., Harriett E., Caroline A., Emily and Charlotte Cleveland. To son Augustus T. Cleveland. All my children to share equally, including John W. and Thomas P. Cleveland. (large estate) Exrs: Brother Wm. L. Cleveland, son-in-law John B. Wilcoxon, Robert W. Quarles. Wit: George Palmer, D.G. Cutting.

Page 156 COFER, JOHN. Nov. 1, 1847. To sons William, Joseph, Joshua, Thomas Cofer. To wife and to the other children. Exr: Son, William H. Cofer. Wit: Robert E. Moss, Samuel T. Burns.

Page 317 COLLEY, FRANCIS. Dec. 1, 1859; June 2, 1862. To wife Frances Colley. To sons: Dempsey, Zebulon D., John Owen Colley, Henry F. Colley; to daus: Sarah A.F. Robert, wife of Milton G. Robert. To each, lands and negroes. To Zebulon when twenty-one years of age. Exrs: Sons. Codicil: To Sarah Frances Colley, dau. of John Owen Colley. Dec. 1859. Exrs: Sons, John Owen Colley & Zebulon Colley: Wit: R. R. Randolph, F. S. Wingfield, Stephen Pettus, A. L. Alexander.

Page 380 COLLEY, SPAIN. Apr. 7, 1856; Dec. 3, 1866. Of advanced age. To wife Nancy Colley the use of all estate. At her death to be divided among my children; John, Sarah, Francis F., Thomas, Caroline, Nancy, Gabriel, Eliza, Martha, H enry and Henrie(ta) Colley. Exrs: Nephew Henry Colley, Milton S. Roberts. Wit: Peter Donelly, Wm. Jones, George E. Harris.

Page 193 COLLINS, GIBSON. July 6, 1852; Aug. 2, 1852. To wife Elizabeth. To dau. Lavinia, wife of Jacob Slack. To dau. Alma, wife of John G. Seal. To dau. Sarah, wife of Barnett Jeter Quinn. Exrs: Sons; John G. Collins, Joseph S. Collins. Wit: Toliver Jones, Charles S. Heard.

Page 171 CORBET, ELEANOR. Jan. 19, 1848; Nov. 6, 1848. To daus: Mary Ann and Amanda M. Taylor. Exrs: Dr. John Pope, A. A. Cleveland. Wit: Solomon J. and Joseph W. Robinson.

Page 276 COX, WM. R. Apr. 30, 1860; June 4, 1860. To wife Sarah J. Cox and her children Elizabeth and Nancy. To brother and his children. To my sisters children: Nancy and Mary Jane Cox. To brother James and Thomas J. Cox. To sister Elizabeth Cosby. To david Cosby. Exr: Wm. E. Reese. Wit: Jas. H. Lane, A. C. McMekin.

Page 43 CREWS, BENEDICTINE. Apr. 16, 1853; July 19, 1841. To gr-dau. Mary Ann Willis, one half of certain property; the other half to John Crews. Legacy to Catharine Dodson. Exr: Lock Weems. Wit: Samuel J. Cassells, Jr., Wm. G. Johnson, Timothy Carrington. Rev. Cassells testified in Bibb Co. Remark: Benedictine, widow of James Crews.

Page 152 DANIEL, JANE E. May 23, 1847; May 26, 1847. To gr. son Andrew C. McJunkin. To gr. dau. Sarah A. McJunkin. To my three gr. children: James C. and Mary J. Goodrum, Emeline E. Goodrum, children of dau. Emeline E. Goodrum. To son Robert C. Daniel, one fourth of my estate. To son Robert C. Daniel to hold in trust for my five gr. children: Andrew C., Sarah A., Samuel, Mary and Robert C. McJunkin. To daughter Mary E. Butler, wife of Edmond M. Butler and her child, one fourth; Edward Butler trustee. To son, Samuel E. Daniel one half of land where I now live, and cash. Exr: Robert C. Daniel. Wit: James T. Harkney, Ambrose J. Bramlett, Samuel Glenn. Ordered to be admitted to record. July 7, 1847. Signed by five Justices of the Court: Lewis S. Brown, A. S. Wingfield, Welcome Fanning, W. Q. Anderson, H . P. Wootten.

Page 105 DANNER, DAVID. Jan. 29, 1844; Nov. 1844. To wife Mary. To dau. Elizabeth. To dau. Sarah, and her son Franklin N. Danner. Exr: Dr. G. F. Buckhannon. Wit: William and Jno. Huguley, Samuel B. Wynn.

Page 265 DEARING, ELIJAH . Dec. 17, 1856; Jan. 9, 1860. To son John B. Dearing, daus. Keziah Hinsman, Marcia Bowen, Lucy Ann Truitt, legacy to each. To gr. dau. Emmie Jackson. Exr: Benjamine A. Hardin. Wit: Samuel Burns, Sr., Wm. A. Burns, Mrs. A. Lynn.

Page 49 DODSON, JOHN C. Proved Jan. 1841. Estate to be divided among my lineal heirs. The share Alexander Brown would be entitled to, in right of his wife. Susan Brown, I give to his dau. Susan. The share William Brown is entitled to, in right of his Mother, Harriett Brown, formerly Harriett Dodson, to be returned to my estate to be divided equally. Mentions lands in Cherokee Co. Exrs: John and Samuel Dodson, Wit: Wm. H. Taylor, Wm. Q. Anderson, W. W. Jordan.

Page 150 DOZIER, ELIZABETH. June 21, 1843; June 8, 1847. To sons Tilman F.

and Ezekiel A. Dozier. To daus. Martha Pounds, Elizabeth Dozier, Jane Gresham, Rebecca Gresham. To gr. dau. Catherine Patnan Dozier. Exr: Tilman F. Dozier. Wit: James Dozier, Henry Massengale, H. L. Embry.

Page 30 DOZIER, JAMES. July 3, 1837; Mch. 18, 1839. To wife Elizabeth Dozier. To son Tilman Dozier. To daus. Martha Travis, Jane Gresham, Sarah Clark, Nancy Droyher. To son-in-law, Marten Webster, to son-in-law Isaac McRory. To son Ezekiel Dozier. To gr. son Warren Alexander Clark, son of Frances Clark, my dau. who is now dead. To William Clark, negroes, etc. To son Tilmon the land whereon I now live, being the same bequeathed to my wife, 392 acres, slaves, etc. To dau. Rebecca Grisom, negroes, furniture, stock, etc. To daus. Martha and Eliza Dozier, Lucretia Webster, and Amanda McRorie. Son Ezekiel and Nancy R. Gresham to be educated. Exrs: Wm. Gresham, Ezekiel Dozier, Wit: T. Kendrick, John Gresham, Henry F. Ellington.

Page 257 DUNAWAY, SAMUEL. June 29, 1858; Nov. 5, 1858. To wife Louisa R. Dunaway. To sons and Daus: Alpheus, Eliza Ann, Henry T., Joseph M. Dearing. To sons H iram D. and William L. Dunaway. To Wm. A. Drake, legatee. Exr: Alpheus Dunaway. Wit: Thos. H. Strothers, David Campbell.

Page 254 DYE, WILLIAM A. May 10, 1852; July 1857. To wife Elizabeth. To dau. Delilah Hopper, wife of Jonathan Hopper. To dau. Sarah Ann Jones, w ife of Arthur Jones. To dau. Nancy Dye and to son W, T. Dye. Exr: Son-in-law Jonathan Hopper. Wit: Lucius Gartrell, John L. Wootten.

Page 221 EDMUND, SARAH R. Oct. 2, 1852; Sept. 5, 1854. To dau. Mary Power, wife of William Power. To dau. Lucinda Power, wife of John Power. To my daus. Parmelia Edmunds and Eliza Silvey, wife of Dolford Silvey. Exr: Samuel Glenn. Wit: Griffin Mathis, Wm. Moore, John H. Mathis.

Page 247 EIDSON, JOHN. Sept. 16, 1856; Oct. 15, 1856. To Eliza Staples, and to four daughters of Edward Waller, "when Eliza Staples marries". Exr: John H. Dyson. Wit: John Q. West, David Fouche, Chas. T. Wingfield.

Page 87 ELLINGTON, THOMAS J. Jan. 17, 1842; Jan. 31, 1843. To bros. Simeon C. and Wm. B., and Tilman Ellington. To my sisters, Elizabeth H. Ellington and Sarah Jane Dillard. Exr: Wm. B. Ellington. Wit: Lock Weems, A. S. Wingfield.

Page 313 EVANS, ARDEN, SR. June 27, 1860; Nov. 27, 1861. To my Mother-in-law Mary Rouss. To nephew and nieces. To Evan Bates son, and his sister H annah Bates. Exrs: Arden Evans, Jr., I. T. Irvin. Wit: T. J. Wall, B. F. Wall.

Page 3 FORMBY, NANCY. Widow, Oct. 12, 1831; Nov. 8, 1836. To Charles

McKnight of Wilkes Co., who married my dau. Susan. To dau. Jincy Whitaker, wife of Abraham Whitaker. To gr. dau. Sarah Ann Whitaker. To dau. Sarah Dawson, wife of Robert Dawson. To dau. Fanny Dawson, wife of Henry T. Dawson. To sons Larkin, Richard, John and Roland Formby. Exrs: William Sherrer, John W. Sherrer, Geo. W. Johnson. Wit: William and John Sherrer, Geo. W. Johnson

Page 40 GARRARD, JOHN. Jan. 14, 1840; May 4, 1840. To wife Martha all of estate with each of my children provided for as she thinks proper. Remainder of estate to be divided equally among my children at death of wife. Exr: Wife. Wit: James N. Wingfield, Augustus W. Flynt.

Page 80 GRAVES, CATHARINE, Jan. 26, 1842; Jan. 31, 1843. To Simeon Hester. To Gr. son James P. Graves. To great grand daughter Catharine Hester. Exr: Simeon Hester. Wit: John and Wm. H. Dyson, L. M. Leonard, Jarvis Seal, Tolison Moorman.

Page 332 GRESHAM, GEORGE, Mch. 8, 1862; April 1863. To wife Nancy S. Gresham. As my children marry, wife to give to each child such property as she can spare. At wife's death, equal division among children. No exr. Wit: A. A. Cleveland, James Harris, G. G. Norman.

Page 293 GRESHAM, KAUFMAN, July 3, 1853; Dec. 11, 1860. To wife Temperance. To children: George, Watson, Margaret Gresham and Winny, wife of Thomas Elliott. To dau. Polly Revier, wife of Hubert B. Revier. To gr. children, Martha Ann, Frances, Susan Paschal Gresham, the children of William Gresham, dec. To Martha Gresham and her child, widow of my son John. To dau. Patience McKenney, widow of George McKinney. Exrs: Sons George, Watson and son-in-law Thomas Elliott. Wit: Lucius Gartrell, Samuel Paschall.

Page 33 GRESHAM, WILLIAM. Nunc. Mch. 18, 1839; Mch. 18, 1839. To wife Jane, all estate. All to be divided equally among my children at wife's death. Wit: H. L. Embry, H. F. Ellington, Jesse Perry, Ezekiel Dozier, John C. Bird.

Page 180 GULLATT, NANCY. Sept. 8, 1850; Mch. 3, 1851. To daus: Nancy Johnson, Rachael Cato. To son George Gullatt. Exrs: Alexander Johnson, Christopher Cato. Wit: John C. McGill, Peter Gullatt.

Page 205 GULLATT, PETER. Jan. 21, 1853; June 1853. To wife Rachael Gullatt. To my children, George and Rebecca Gullatt. Exrs: Son George and my wife. Wit: William D. Quinn, Alex. Frazier, Wm. Gullatt.

Page 46 HANSON, ELIZABETH. Nov. 9, 1838; Jan. 28, 1841. To niece Elizabeth Knox. To Caroline Knox. To Jane Sutton, formerly Jane Knox. To Elizabeth Warren, formerly Elizabeth Knox. To Elizabeth Knox and her three daus:

Caroline, Jane and Elizabeth. To Ann Dodson, formerly Ann Knox, dau. of Elizabeth Knox. To William Dodson, son of Charles and Ann Dodson. To Elizabeth Hanson, dau. of John M. Hanson, dec. To Sarah Hanson, dau. of John M. Hanson, dec. To John Hanson, son of John, dec. To Walter H. Weems and brother Lock Weems. Exr: Lock Weems. Wit: G. L. Rakestraw, A. S. Wingfield, E. M. Burton.

Page 196 HARRIS, MARY. Jan. 19, 1849; Sept. 6, 1852. Mentions deceased dau. Rebecca Roberts. To my gr. son James J. Harris. To my dau. Caroline Fluker's children. To daus. of Nancy Waters. To Jacob Kendricks two daughters, Mary Ann and Susan. Exr: Son James Harris. Wit: Edward Waller, John H. Dyson. Codicil: To gr. son James J. Harris. To my gr. daus. Cornelia Mary Harris and Eva Clifford Harris. To my gr. son David Ellington. Date of Codicil, June 7, 1852.

Page 36 HATCHETT, EDWARD. Feb. 27, 1839; Nov. 4, 1839. All estate to be kept together for use of wife and support of children. Wife, Harriett. Wit: Henry and Sarah Poss, Susan Ogden, Nuc. No exrs.

Page 206 HEARD, JESSE, OF Mis issippi. July 2, 1853; Aug. 5, 1853. To my mother Mrs. Caroline Heard. To brothers Frances, Faulkner, Stephen and Benjamine. To sisters Caroline, Henrietta, Judith, Eliza Heard all of Wilkes Co. Ga. To cousin Reuben Smith, cash. To my brother William S. Heard. To my sister Ann W. Bradley $5000.00. Exr: Brother, Wm. S. Heard. Wit: Purnal and James R. Truett, Gilchrist Jones.

Page 190 HENDERSON, HELEN B. June 6, 1849; Mch. 1, 1852. To my Father Elijah Dearing. To brother John B. Dearing. To my three sisters: Marcia Bowen, Lucy Ann Truitt, Keziah Hindsman. Exr: Gideon Norman. Wit: Enoch Callaway, John and Lucy Huguley.

Page 65 HENDERSON, JOSEPH. Jan. 10, 1840; June 3, 1842. Mentions dec'd. wife Peggy Henderson. To sons Mitchell, Joseph, Felix G., Jesse M. and Richard Henderson. To dau. Nancy Lyon, land in Wilkinson Co. To gr. son Joseph Malone. To gr. dau. Hazeltine Malone. To my gr. children by son Simeon Henderson, dec. To the children of my son Richard Henderson, dec. Mentions dau. Araminta Malone, dec. Legacy to her children. Exrs: Sons Mitchell and Felix Henderson. Wit: Enoch Callaway, J. W. Jackon, Christopher Binns. (This will was recorded). A second will follows, in which testator mentions deceased wife Peggy Henderson. Mentions all his claim in estate of Elijah Dearing, such property as may be divided between his widow: Nancy M. Dearing, and the heirs of Elijah Dearing, dec. To son Felix G., the plantation whereon I live, 800 acres, with all appurtenances. To wife Helen B. Henderson, all my claim to estate of Elijah Dearing. Mentions deceased wife Nancy M. Dearing and gr. child Joseph H. Malone. Mentions the grave of Peggy Henderson. Signed Jan. 3, 1842, proved June 3, 1842.

Page 110 to 118 HILL, WYLIE. Feb. 13, 1837; July 20, 1844. To youngest sons Wylie P. and Abraham T. W. Hill, at majority. To the children of son Burwell P. Hill, by Martha, my last wife. To Sarah Ann Eliza Render Hill. dau. of my first wife. To children of Lodowick M. Hill that are married: Burwell, Lodowick, Sarah C. M. Johnson, Martha P. DuBose, Tabitha M. Duncan. To my wife Martha. Mentions Wm. Rivers, Legatee. Exrs: Sons Lodowick, Wylie, Abraham as they become of age. Wit: T. J. Walton, Thomas Christian, Thomas B. Hill. Codicil: In which he mentions he had already given eight of his children property. Dates of Codicil: Jan. 28, 1845; April 7, 1844.

Page 183 HILLHOUSE, DAVID P. Mch. 10, 1851; July 24, 1851. To A. L. Alexander; to Lock Weems. To Mrs. Ann E. Shepherd and her two children Sarah P. and William Shepherd: To Edward T. Shepherd and brother A. H aygood Shepherd. To Theodore Stark and Misses Martha T., and Emma and Mary Stark. To Mrs. Eliza Herriott and to Mrs. Harriett Glennie. To Mrs. Sarah Means, wife of General John H. Means. To Elisha & Abigail Porter & their sister Mrs. Permelia Smith. To Thomas Hillhouse Schuyler and sisters Caroline and Sarah Schuyler. To Caroline & Elizabeth Bellamy. Exr: Alexander R. Lawton. Wit: Thomas Semmes, E. M. Burton.

Page 142 HINTON, JAMES. To wife Sally certain property; at her death to revert to my youngest heirs; Emma Louisa and Clary Ann Hinton. To six eldest children: John T. Wootten's wife; Jesse Hinton; Fielding Lewis Hinton's children; wife of Henry P. Wootten; wife of William L. Wootten; Elizabeth Hinton Peters; Sarah A. Hinton. Henry P. Wootten, gdn. of youngest. Exrs: Henry Wootten, Samuel Danforth. Wit: N. N. Howard, Benj.Smith, J.P. "Proved June 10, 1846".

Page 70 H OLLIDAY, ALLEN. Oct. 1, 1841; Mch. 1842. To wife Nancy. Mentions lands in Cherokee, Dooly and Wilkes Counties. To sons William and Mariah Elliott. James R. Elliott agent. To Miss Nancy Holliday. To my three daus. Lavinia Camilla Holliday, Syncha R. Holliday, and Frances Adelaide E. Holliday, at death of their Mother. To my four gr. children, Martha Ann Paschal, Amelia Paschal, Mary Jane Paschal minors, their Father John L. Paschal. Exrs: Wife, Allen and William Holliday. Wit: R. Booker, Geo. Poss, Thomas Holliday.

Page 198 HOPKINS, ISAAC. June 15, 1850; Dec. 6, 1852. To son George Hopkins, and to his son John G. Hopkins for his Mother, Mary Hopkins. Exr: Lemuel B. Wynn. Wit: William and John T. Huguely.

Page 157 HUGULEY, ALLEY. July 8, 1840; Dec. 15, 1847. To gr. daus. Elizabeth Ann and Eliza Dallas. To friend Kitty Wynn. To Sarah Ann Hathcock. To sons: John, Zachariah, Amos, George Huguley. To daus. Polly Ross and Nancy wife of Lloyd Cooper. To Alley Cooper, dau. (wife of Joseph Cooper). To Sackfield Walker, Exrs: Sons. Wit: Thomas C. Marchall, Geo. F. Buckhannon, Wm. and Benajah Prather.

Page 45 HUGULEY, REBECCA. Apr. 16, 1835; Nov. 2, 1840. To son John Huguley. To dau. Rebecca Thornton. To exrs: Wit: Peter and Alexander Gullatt.

Page 243 IRVIN, ISAIAH T. SR. Mch. 3, 1856; Apr. 20, 1856. To wife Isabella. To gr. son John Pope Johnson. To dau. Louisa Crosby and husband Bayless R. Crosby. To gr. daus. Caroline Favor, Ann Reese, Isabella Askew. To gr. sons Isaiah T. Davis, Andrew J. Davis. To sons Isaiah T. Irvin, Jr. and Charles M. Irvin. To gr. dau. Martha J. L. Stephens. To daus. Nancy M. Favor, Martha S. Battle and Mary A. Callaway and her children. To Isabella Bacon, John H. Walton and Wm. S. Walton. Exrs: Sons Charles and Isaiah T. Irvin. Wit: L. M. Huff, Andrew Evans, James H. Lane.

Page 286 IRVIN, I. T. See Page 59.

Page 256 JACKSON, SARAH . No date. Sept. 6, 1856. To sons John F. and Matthew Jackson. To dau. Nancy M. Short, husband John Short. Exrs: Son John F. Jackson. My brother Thomas Favor, Isiah T. Irvin, Jr. Wit: Daniel M. Irvin, Isaiah T. Favor.

Page 25 JARRATT, ATHALI. July 28, 1826. To Peter Bennett in trust for my dau. Sarah Hurley; after her death, to her children. To dau. Frances Bennett, negroes, etc. At her death to go to Nancy Ogletree and her heirs. Wit: Daniel Low. Alfred S. Boren. (Will cancelled). Estate Records filed in Wilkes County.

Page 204 JARRETT, JOHNSON TERRELL. Jan. 7, 1853; Jan. 22, 1853. To wife Malinda Jarrett. To sisters Louisa Arnold of Taliaferro Co., and Sophronia Borum of Randolph Co., Ga. Exrs: Brother Geo. W. Jarrett and wife. Wit: J. J. Robertson, A. C. Hanson, James Smith.

Page 191 JOHNSON, JACOB. Feb. 10, 1851; Jan. 8, 1852. To my children: Charles M. Johnson, Cincinatus Johnson, Malinda Jarrott. To children of son Charles: Algernon, Alphonso, Alonzo and Rebecca and infant, not named. No executor. Wit: James Tinsley, John Wright.

Page 134 JONES, SAMUEL. Aug. 23, 1840; Nov. 5, 1845. To Sarah A. Slaton and Mary A. Slaton, daus. of Wm. Slaton. To William Slaton of Wilkes Co. in trust for Samuel Jones Slaton, son of Zachariah Slaton. To Samuel Jones Cooper, son of Newton D. Cooper. To Martha A. Reese. To Mary L. Flynt. To Samuel Jones Harkry, son of Daniel Harkry. To Amanda T. Flynt. To Samuel Jones Slaton, son of Columbus Slaton. To Sarah Ann Haynes, dau. of Lucy Haynes. To Braxton Bird of Monroe Co. To Henry and Wm. Slaton, sons of Samuel Slaton. To Susan Twadly Tweedley, sister of Henry and Wm. Slaton. To Wm. Slaton of Wilkes Co. in trust for Elizabeth Bryant, five hundred dollars yearly; after her death to go to Mrs. Lucy Haynes. To wife Amelia

C. Jones; after wife's death, one fifth part of the whole estate to go to James H. Flynt and his children; to Augustus Flynt and his children, one fifth; To Virginia C. Shehan and her children, one fifth. To heirs of Elvira T. Wright, dec. one fifth. Exrs: James H. Flynt, Gainham Rakestraw. Wit: Benj. Wallace, S. R. Crenshaw, James Hackney. Codicil: To George Flynt; to Sarah Amelia Flynt, dau. of Jas. H. Flynt. To Sarah A. Haynes, S. H. Slaton, Mary A. Slaton and Newton D. Cooper and Virginia O. Shehan my plantation in Taliaferro Co. That Jas. H. Flynt is to buy a plantation for the children of Newton Cooper of Taliaferro Co. and when children become of age, to belong to them. Date of Codicil, Nov. 3, 1843.

Page 24 JONES, THOMAS. Mar. 3, 1838; Sept. 5, 1838. To sons Joseph T. and James Augustus Jones. To wife Martha. To my youngest children, Samuel, Thomas Welch, Mary Frances, Wm. Robertson and Benjamine Welch. When Samuel arrives at age of twenty-one, the remainder of my estate to be divided equally. Exr: Wife. In case of her death Mr. Adam Alexander, exr. Children to be educated respectibly and in a most Christain like manner. Wit: F. Ficklen, A. L. Lewis, Joseph Mosely.

Page 239 JORDAN, JOHN. No date. Apr. 2, 1856. To son Benjamine F. Jorden, all estate. If I should die childless, I give my cook woman to my sister Mary Walker; balance of negroes put into lots by families, and divided among my brother Mathew (with exception of his son Wm. F. Jordan as he has a professional education) and bro. Edwin Jorden, and my sister Mary Walker's children, with exception of her son, Wm. F. Walker as he has been provided for. If any of my negroes wish to be sold, to stay with their families, let them be sold. No Exrs. Wit: N. W. Taliaferro, John L. Wootten.

Page 182 KAPPLE, DIANA M. No date. Proved July term 1851. To sons Benjamine and Michael Kapple. Exr. Wm. Reese. Wit: John H. Pope, G. Wingfield.

Page 128 KENDRICK, JONES. Jan. 15, 1845; Mch. 1845. To Edward R. Anderson. To sons; John R. Kendrick, Greene M. Kendrick and Wm. W. Simpson equal shares. To children, John B. Jones, Susan Simpson, Tabitha J. Simpson, the wife of William W. Simpson. To son Tilman Kendrick. To gr. children, the children of Susannah Simpson. To gr. dau. Mary Carter. Exrs: Son Martin Kendrick, son Edward R. Anderson and John R. Kendrick; Wm. R. Simpson guardian of son Green M. Kendrick. Wit: John Q. West, J. E. Penrose.

Page 154 KILGORE, MARY T. Mch. 1, 1845; Sept. 1847. To sons Charles A. and Wm. S. Kilgore, all estate. Exr: Wm. Q. Anderson, Codicil: To dau. drawn by Benajah and Wm. Kilgore. Same Exr. Wit: Geo. Wolf, Wm. Huguley, Geo. F. Buckhannon. Codicil date, Apr. 5, 1847.

Page 39 KILGORE, WILLIAM. Dec. 1, 1839. Jan. 6, 1840. To son Charles Kilgore. To wife for her use and for support of my children. My two youngest children,

William G. and Mary Ann to be educated. Exr: Wife, Mary T. Kilgore. Wit: Robert Toombs, John H. Dyson, Wm. L. Anderson.

Page 125 KING, MARY. To two daus. Martha Colley, Martha Brooks, (widow) all my lands in Wilkes Co. To daus: Rachael Kent, Elizabeth Wise, Margaret Jackson, and Sarah, her husband's name I know not. Exrs: Martha Colley, Mary Brooks. Wit: Jacob Hubbard, Newton D. Armour.

Page 94 LANDRUM, JOHN. Sept. 24, 1843; Nov. 6, 1843. To wife Lettice. To my three gr. children: Sarah, Margaret and John Fortson, lands in Early Co. and in Cherokee Co. Estate to be divided equally. Exr: William Cade. Wit: A. T. Stokes, F. E. Smith.

Page 77 LEVERETT, ANN. July 19, 1830; Nov. 21, 1842. To gr. children of my dau. Amanda Moorman, wife of Wm. Moorman. To my three gr. children of my dau. Eliza and Thomas J. Booker: Eliza Ann, Wm. R. and James Booker, one fifth part of my estate. To dau. Tenery, wife of George Shank, one fifth part. To children of my dau. Adeline Jones, wife of Wm. Jones. To dau. Mary Leverett, now single. Exr: George Shank. Wit: Peter Lamar, Ezekiel Lamar, Thos. Jennings.

Page 68 LINDSEY, JAMES. Jan. 14, 1842; July 7, 1842. To wife Letitia Lindsey all estate. Mentions Cherokee Co. lands, to be sold, After death of wife, all property to be equally divided among my children: James M. Lindsey, Martha J. Sutton (?), Willis H. Lindsey, William Lindsey, John T. Lindsey, and the children of Mary Slack, wife of John Slack, and the children of Eliza Hay formerly Eliza Lindsey, now wife of Isaac Lindsey and her children, if any. The children of Mary Slack to draw one seventh part and the children of Eliza Lindsey Hay, and of Isaac Lindsey. Exr: Wife Letitia, son Willis H. Lindsey and Henry P. Wootten. Wit: Henry P. Wootten, James M. Lindsey.

Page 214 LINDSEY, LETITIA. Feb. 3, 1854; Mch. 6, 1854. To Mother Mary Bostick. To son-in-law William Sutton. To my three sons: James M., William B., John T. Lindsey. To dau. Mary Slack and Eliza H ay. Exrs: Sons Willis H. and John T. Lindsey, son-in-law Wm. Sutton. Wit: E. W. Anderson, W. D. Quinn, Wm. P. Bradford.

Page 296 McKINNEY, GEORGE. June 15, 1858; Jan. 22, 1861. To wife Fanny. To gr. son George Edward Strozier, and my gr. children Jane, Augustus, Mary, William, Margaret, the children of my departed son William McKenney. To dau. Margaret Burdette. To sons Patrick and Cicero. To daus. J. Elizabeth Overton and Louisa McKenney. Exr: Son John. Wit: John Q. West, Patrick J. Barnett.

Page 89 McRAE, NANCY A. Feb. 18, 1843; Aug. 7, 1843. To John Landrum and wife Lettice. To three gr. children: Sarah, Margaret and John Fortson. Exr: William Cade. Wit: A. T. Stokes, F. E. Smith, James Henly. Codicil: To my nieces son, Wm.H. Aughtry: To my niece's dau. Mary E. Blair, wife of James Blair and her children: To niece's dau. Josephine A. Aughtry and her heirs. To Nancy Pomroy, twelve hundred dollars. Mentions silver, jewelry, gold snuff box, minature of Brother Henry and Father's Family Bible. Gifts to Presbyterian Church. To friend, James M. Smith, my walnut dressing table. Exrs: Lewis S. Brown, John Dyson. Wit: W. F. Baker, John Jesse, James M. Smith. Signed Mch. 10, 1843.

Page 54 to 59 MERCER, REV. JESSE. June 3, 1841; Nov. 1, 1841. To beloved Wife Nancy. All my servants to be sold in mercy, that is, to give them time to find masters - such masters as may be desireable to them. (This will very lengthy). Testator bequeaths property to Baptist Publication Society and to numerous societies and Institutions. To American Foreign Mission Societies, to the American Baptist Home Missions of Georgia. To Colleges, to Baptist Convention Societies, etc. To Mercer University, Trustees, Penfield, Greene Co. To brother Joshua of Randolph Co. and of Baker Co., personalty . My Library to Mercer University. This will declared void by Jesse Mercer. The same will approximately, with addition to Mercer University fund in which amount is set aside constituting annuity funds for the Professorship of Sacred Biblical Literature or Theological Learning. Exrs: David E. Butler, Dr. Fielding Ficklen, Wm. F. Baker. Wit: A. S. Wingfield, John Pettus.

Page 20 MONTGOMERY, MARY. Jan. 1838; May 7, 1838. To David Montgomery, Sr. To dau. Elizabeth Robinson, one sixth of my estate after paying a note given by James Robinson. To Nancy Montgomery and her children. To Elizabeth Lee, dau. of Daniel Arnold. To Mary McGehee. To Sarah White, dau. of James White, each to receive one sixth part. Exr: William Simpson, William Slaton. Wit: Frances Slaton, James T. Hackney.

Page 304 MOORE, ELIZABETH. Nov. 1, 1858; June 4, 1861. That part of my estate that might fall to the children of John H. More (Moore) my deceased son, I bequeath to my son William Moore. Remainder of my estate to be equally divided among my heirs. Exrs: Brother Aristides Callaway, Wm. M. Reese. Wit: Van A. Echols, Edward F. and Alex. Echols.

Page 240 MOSS, ELIZABETH V. July 23, 1854; Apr. 1, 1854. Of Lincoln Co., to gr. son Rachael Dunston Blackwell, Samuel L. Wynn, gdn. To son David M. Moss. To dau. Jane Wynn and Sarah Wingfield, equal shares with David Moss, Sarah's son by first marriage to Asbury Tate, to be included with her other children. Exrs: A. S. Wingfield, Samuel Wynn. Wit: Toliver Jones, Wm. D. Quinn.

Page 253 MURPHEY, JANE. Feb. 1857; May 4, 1857. To nieces George Ann Murphey,/ Exrs: Friends, C. H. Bussey, A. J. Paschal. Wit: A. J. Paschal, Mary Jane and Mary Tom Murphey.

Page 187 MURPHEY, JOHN. Dec. 31, 1851; Feb. 21, 1852. To wife Almeda. To sisters Jane and Rebecca Murphey. Mentions his wife's three children: Georgia Ann, Martha Jane, Mary Tom Murphey. Exrs: Wife and Joseph Holiday. Wit: John L. Paschal, David Campbell.

Page 176 MURPHEY, LUCY. May 21, 1850; July 1, 1850. To daus: Emaline Agee, Amanda Thornton. To children: John L. and William Francis Murphey, Lucy Smith, Almeda Burdett, Lucy Sanders. To gr. dau. Lucy Poss. To Mother Lucy Simpson. Exrs: Allen T. Holliday, Wm. M. Booker. Wit: G. G. Norman. C. C. O.

Page 249 NOLAN, JAMES. June 12, 1856; Dec. 12, 1856. To sons James, Thomas, John H. Nolan. To my dau. Francis Huguley. To dau. Polly Bolton and Nancy West. Exrs: Son-in-law, John West, William H. Huguley son James Nolan. Wit: Thos. P. Burdett, A. C. McMekin. (Valuable estate).

Page 81 NORMAN, ARGYLE. Mch. 6, 1840; Jan. 26, 1843. To wife Mary P. Norman, who is to take charge of my estate, with John L. Wynn as my exr. Wife to keep estate together for the support and education of my children. When all children become of age, equal division, her six children included. Wit: John and Wm. Dyson.

Page 131 NORMAN, ELIZABETH. Sept. 25, 1838; Oct. 8, 1845. To children: Moses Sutton, John Sutton, Wm. P. Muse, Jackson Muse, Mary Jackson and the minor children of dau. Nancy Sutton, but at time of her death was wife of Presley Aycock. To dau. Elizabeth Muse and my gr. son John Muse. Exrs: Moses Sutton, Joseph Jackson. Wit: Wm. Hudspeth, Stephen A. Johnson, Wm. J. Spratlin.

Page 7 NORMAN, JESSE. Nov. 17, 1836; Mch. 25, 1837. To daus. Frances Shumate and Elizabeth Norman, legacy in trust. To sons Willis R. Norman, William S. Norman, Jeremiah B. Norman, Jesse M. Norman. To gr. dau. Sarah Frances Baird. To wife Elizabeth. Exrs: Willis R., Wm. S., and Jeremiah B. Norman. Wit: Henry P. Wootten, Thomas Wootten.

Page 120 OGLESBY, GARRETT. Mch. 11, 1843; July 15, 1845. To wife, not named. Mentions his two youngest sons, Junius S. and Temus W., minors who are to be educated. To dau. Mary L. Oglesby. After death of wife, estate to be divided among my children; George J., Martha E., Mary L., Minor T., Shaler H., Junius S., Temus W., Joseph L. Oglesby and the children of my sons Urbane B. and Thos. J. Oglesby and the children of my dau. Lucy Christian Smith. Exrs: Joseph L. Oglesby, Thomas Wootten. Wit: Nimrod Waller, Wm. B. Norman, W. N. Jorden.

Page 10 OWENS, MARY. Oct. 24, 1836; July 21, 1837. To gr. sons Owen and Thomas Shearman. To the children of my dau. Frances Colley; Henry F. Colley, Dempsey C. Colley, Sarah Ann Colley, Zebulon C., John O.Colley their father Francis Colley. To daus. Jemima Shearman, Frances Colley and children of Jemima Shearman, all the balance of household furniture. Exr: Son-in-law Francis Colley. Wit: Sims L. Brown, William Kilgore, R. J. Willis.

Page 305 PALMER, GEORGE W. Apr. 19, 1861; Aug. 6, 1861. To wife Sarah E. W. Palmer. To sons: Stephen R., George and John T. Palmer. Exrs: Robert H. Vickers, Stephen R. Palmer. Wit: Sam Barnett, John D. Smith, O. L. Battle.

Page 95 PARKINSON, LEVIN. Dec. 25, 1843; May 27, 1844. To son-in-law Samuel Dunaway. To son John Parkinson. To my three daus. Nancy Miller, Rachael Bentley, Harriett Jefferson. To Peggy McElroy. To my five unmarried children: Zadock, Sarah, Elizabeth, Rhods, Rebecca, Artimesary Parkinson. Exr: Richard J. Holliday. Wit: John P. Baird, Griffin Tankersley.

Page 219 PASCHAL, SAMUEL. May 8, 1845; July 10, 1854. To sons A. J. Paschal, Dennis, Harris and E. Paschal. To Edward and Joseph M. Gillespie, grand sons. Exrs: A. J., Dennis Paschal. Wit: Allen Holliday, Dennis Paschal, Sr., C. H. Bussey.

Page 52 PELOT, JOHN F. Jan. 23, 1841; no probate date. To wife Harriett L. my property in Washington. To friend Mary Minton, my property in South Carolina. To son Francis L. Pelot. Remainder to wife and the children I have by her. Exrs: Edward M. Burton, Henry Pope. Wit: H. M. Clark, E. A. Smith, Robert Toombs.

Page 123 PETEET, CHENOTH. Jan. 28, 1845; July 25, 1845. To wife Patsy and to my youngest unmarried children. Exr: Wife. Wit: James R. Lockett, Parker Callaway. Codicil: Gifts to eldest dau. Susan D. Lawrence. Signed Apr. 7, 1845.

Page 229 PETEET, ELIZABETH. Dec. 31, 1844; Apr. 12, 1855. To dau. Lucinda Watkins, to gr. dau. Eliza Ann Jackson. To son, John R. Peteet. Exr: Son-in-law Benjamine Watkins: Wit: Royland Beasley, A. S. Wingfield.

Page 175 PETTUS, JOHN. July 9, 1849; Nov. 5, 1849. To wife. To daus. Elizabeth Walton, Caroline Pettus, Mary Lane, Mary Pettus. Exrs: Wife and Wm. Reese. Wit: John H. Burks, F. W. Darracott.

Eliza Ann Jackson

1860 John H Pope

1835 Stovall Pool daughter Eliza Ann Jackson Pool

Page 300 PETTUS, STEPHEN G. June 13, 1856; May 6, 1861. To daus. Mary Ann Pettus, $20,000. To my son Stephen G. Pettus. To gr. son Stephen Robert Palmer. To gr. dau. Sarah Palmer. To son-in-law George W. Palmer. To wife, not named. Exrs: Son-in-law Geo. Palmer, son Stephen G. Pettus. Wit: G. P. Cozart, Wm. Reese.

Page 5 POOL, STOVALL. Aug. 26, 1835; Feb. 21, 1837. To dau. Eliza Ann Jackson. To son John Pool, minor. To wife Mary. Dau. Bonita Davis has received her share. Exr: James Huling. Wit: James T. Hay, A. G. Semmes, Wm. D. Harris.

Page 288 POPE, JOHN H. Nov. 4, 1859; Dec. 22, 1860. To sons Barton Chapman Pope. William Henry Pope. Exr: Brother Alexander Pope. Wit: R. H. Vickers. Garnett Andrews, William A. Pope. Codicil: To all my children in Texas. To all my gr. children in Texas and Florida. To son Alex. and his children. To my sons-in-law, Richard and Iverson Lane, and to their children. Exrs: Son George and Benjamine Pope. Apr. 27, 1860.

Page 87 POPE, MARY. May 4, 1840; July 3, 1843. To gr. son Wylie M. Pope. To gr. son Augustus Huling. To dau. Sarah Huling. To gr. son Wylie H. Pope. Exrs: Nicholas M. Taliaferro, Thos. Wootten. Wit: Wesley P. Arnold, Wm. H. Jenison.

Page 29 POSS, WILLIAM. Dec. 27, 1838; Mch. 4, 1839. To wife Elizabeth Poss, all estate. All my children to inherit equal shares. Exr: Felix Shank. Wit: John Moreman, Thomas Elliott.

Page 274 POWELL, MARY. Feb. 18, 1850; Apr. 2, 1860. To Elizabeth Burdett, wife of Joseph T. Burdett. To Augustine C. McMekin. Exr: John H. Dyson. Wit: Austin C. McMekin, Thos. P. Burdett.

Page 16 PRATHER, ELIAS J. Oct. 5, 1837; Nov. 6, 1837. Requests his wife to move to Harris Co and settle on his land there. Taliaferro Willis to take the two boys and manage their property. Wife and children to share equally. Exrs: Wife and Taliaferro Willis. Wit: Augustine D. Statham, John C. Stokes, Wm. H. Freeman.

Page 200 PULLEN, JAMES. Apr. 20, 1852; Jan. term 1853. To my wife and to each of my children equal shares, after fifteen years. Exr: None. Wit: John W. Rhodes, Wm. D. Quinn.

Page 132 QUIGLEY, CHARLES. Oct. 15, 1845; Oct. 1853. To son Charles Quigley in trust for his children. To son Wm. A. Quigley in trust for his children. Wife to have a life interest in estate. Mentions five unmarried daughters - not named. Exrs: Charles M. and B. Quigley. Wit: Lewis S. Brown, A. J. Wingfield.

Page 73 RAKESTRAW, ANN S. Nov. 1836; Aug. 2, 1842. To John H. Dyson, in trust, for the sole use of my husband Gainham L. Rakestraw, certain property. Exr: John H. Dyson. Wit: Lucy T. Montgomery, Nathan Truitt.

Page 178 RANDOLPH, DOROTHY. Sept. 8, 1849; Mch. 3, 1857. To daus. Mariah J. Randolph. To gr. daus. Jacintha Dorothy Randolph, Isabella Randolph, at division of estate of Richard Randolph, dec. Nov. 1844. Thomas P. Randolph, Martha P. Triplett, Robert R. Randolph, Isabella, Edmond, Louisa Maria, Jacinthy Dorothy, Thomas, Richard, the children of my son Richard H. Randolph, dec. Exr: Mariah J. Randolph, dau. Wit: J. J. Robinson, George H. Petrie.

Page 202 RANDOLPH, ROBERT R. Dec. 23, 1853; Jan. 10, 1853. To wife Mary A. Randolph. To sons Robert H. and Clifton Randolph, minors. Exr: James F. Hamilton. Wit: George W. Palmer, Stephen G. Pettus, John Jesse.

Page 199 RAY, MARY. Mch. 17, 1843; Jan. term 1853. Of advanced age. To my daus: Emily Harris and Amanda Baily. To son John Ray. To gr. son John A. Ray. Exrs: Son-in-law, Elbert G. Harris, Ephraim Bailey. Wit: F. C. Wingfield, James and Jno. Bentley.

Page 371 REVIERE, HERBERT. Mch. 10, 1864; Mch. 16, 1864. To wife Polly. To my three youngest daus: Martha Jane, Mary Frances, Sarah Cornelia Reviere. To my other children William A. Reviere and his children. To James Reviere and his children. To John K. Reviere and his children. To George G. Reviere and his children. To Patience L. Jacobs and her children. To Sarah C. Reviere. Sons: Wm. A., and George G., and James J. to have use of their children's shares. Exrs: Wife, and son-in-law, W. G. Jacobs. Wit: John M. Ivy, E. Waller, Henry Thompson.

Page 315 RHODES, SAMUEL. Apr. 23, 1862; June 2, 1862. To wife Esther. That part which would come to Joseph Rhodes, to go to his children by his wife Catharine Rhodes. Exr: Wife and son William. Wit: Sam Barnett, F. C. Armstrong.

Page 230 ROBINSON, JOSEPH W. Sept. 19, 1853; Apr. 4, 1855. To wife Caroline. To my children: Alexander Webster Robinson, Llewellyn and Laura Robinson, John Joseph Robinson. To my son Francis James Robinson. Exr: Son Francis James Robinson. Wit: James E. Waddy, Wm. D. Hamilton.

Page 233 ROSE, CATHERINE. Sept. 7, 1844; July 24, 1855. To my Father

Henry Rose. To Mother Elizabeth Rose. To nephew James H. Combs. To brother-in-law Thomas H. Marlow. To sister Ann Marlow. To nieces: Sarah J. Marlow and Catherine R. Marlow. To nephew John T. Marlow. Exr: My Father, Henry Rose. Wit: James W. Dyson, John D. Cooper.

Page 17 RUDDLE, LEE ANN. Nov. 25, 1833; Jan. 1, 1838. To Wm. Dearing and Alexander Pope. In trust for my gr-dau. Cordelia Charlton. To gr-dau. Mary Charlton. Sister of Cordelia. Mentions dau. who resides in Athens who married Mr. Stanford. Leaves her faithful old negro woman free. Exr: Wit: Nancy W. Stone, Wm. Jones, Frances Lipman, James W. Price.

Page 41 SAFFOLD, REUBEN. Jan. 14, 1840; Jan. 18, 1840. In presence of Thomas Blakey, Thomas R. Thrumond and Martha Saffold, he gives negroes to his Mother's family. To youngest brother, the negro Ludlow. To wife Amanda all estate. No. Exrs.

Page 164 SANDIFER, SUSAN. May 13, 1848; July 3, 1848. To James H. Price. To Ann Eliza Price. Friend, Mrs. Sarah Robert. The land in Cherokee Co., and remainder of my estate, I give to children of Dr. James Price, by his wife Susan H . Price. No Exrs: Wit: Nathaniel Snelson, Sarah A. T. Moon (or Moore).

Page 21 SANDEFORD, HARRIS. Aug. 30, 1829; Sept. 3, 1838. To my Father, not named - to sister Susan. To nieces Lucy and Susan Johnson, who are unmarried. Exrs: Lewis G. Brown, John H. Dyson. Wit: James M. Anderson, Thomas A. Carter.

Page 148 SHANK, HENRY. Nov. 8, 1846; Mch. term 1847. To wife Susannah, all estate. To sons Felix, George F., Henry M. minors. To daus. America, Caroline Frances, Cordelia and Susan Shank. To dau. Delia Wellmaker, wife of Israel Wellmaker. To dau. Elizabeth, wife of Felix Wellmaker. To dau. Mary Shank. Exrs: Wife and Felix Shank, and testators brother, George Shank. Wit: Elias Wellmaker, John O. Ferrell, Alex. Frazer.

Page 37 SHUMATE, CATHERINE. May 30, 1835; July 25, 1839. To legal heirs of my gr. son John B. Leonard; Thomas Fleming Leonard; minors; Samuel Edward Leonard; Ludwell M. Leonard; John B. Leonard. To dau. Polly Wood. To Drury Wood, cash. Exr: Gr. son John B. Leonard. Wit: John R. Anderson, R. H. Wilkes, Lewis S. Brown.

Page 12 SMITH, EBENEZER. Feb. 13, 1837; July 3, 1837. To daus: Mary Walton, Ann E. Thurmond, Frances Thurmond, Sarah Jane Smith. To sons Reuben Smith, Francis E. Smith. To wife Fanny the plantation on which I live and all household effects. To gr. son Francis E. Smith. Mentions land in Cherokee Co., and in Wilkinson Co. which was drawn by his Father Francis Smith. Exr: William D. Anderson, Wit: Elizabeth Williams, Thomas Anderson, Thomas Wootten.

Page 172 STAPLES, JOHN. Nunc. Apr. 26, 1849; May 7, 1849. All property of every description to wife for her to use for jount benefit and support of self and daughter Sarah, until she arrives at lawful age or marries; to be divided equally, at wife's death, between dau. Sarah and David Cosby. At Sarah's death to her children. No Exrs: James Harris, David Cosby, Tilman Dozier, witnesses.

Page 195 STANDARD, DANIEL. May 2, 1852; Sept. 1852. To wife Ann H. Standard. To son John T. Standard. Mentions his minor children, to be educated - not named. Exr: Son John T. Standard. Wit: John M. Booker, Kimbro S. Turner.

Page 165 STOKES, SARAH. Sept. 24, 1845; Oct. 2, 1848. To daus. Mary and Elizabeth Stokes and the children of my son Micajah T. Anthony of Wilkes Co. All my negroes to be equally divided between Mary, Elizabeth and the children of Micajah T. Anthony, except four negroes not included: I want them to choose which legatees they prefer: When unable to work, to be comfortably maintained. To William A. Stokes, cash at majority. To gr. son John A. Stokes the land whereon his Father Armistead T. Stokes now resided in Wilkes, on Broad River. The rest of my land of one thousand and one hundred acres on Pistol Creek, with all things on the plantation except my carriage horses and carriage, to be sold and used for education of my gr. son John A. Stokes and for his Father's benefit. The house and lot I live on to be sold and proceeds divided I give my land on Greenboro Road, also all my plate of every kind, candlesticks, spoons, etc. Silver tea and coffee sets, castors to Eliza T. Hunt. Mahongany furniture to Mary and Eliza and to gr. son John A. Stokes and furniture to gr. dau. Sarah M. Herring. To my dau.Mary Herring my carriage and horses. The rest of the furniture to children of Micajah T. Anthony. Exrs: Not named. Wit: F. Ficklen, Henry Terrell, A. S. Wingfield. J. I. C.

Page 207 STONE, WILLIAM. Mch. 15, 1853; Nov. 7, 1853. Of the town of Washington, Wilkes Co. To dau. Margaret Carter. To dau. Mary Octavia Wingfield, and Clara Augusta Harmon. All estate to wife Mary Stone. At wife's death equal shares to son Wm. A. Stone, Esther Ann Mahoney, Emma Frances Dearing, Margaret C. Stone, Mary O. Wingfield and Clara A. Harmon. Exrs: Wife and son-in-law James J. Harman. Wit: Stephen G. Pettus, Lewis S. Brown.

Page 159 STRIBLING, THOMAS. Apr. 6, 1847; Jan. 10, 1848. To wife Sarah, to sons Charles C., William F., Milton O., Thomas L. Stribling. To dau. Sarah Jones and Frances A. Stribling. To son Augustine E. Stribling. To Isaac McLendon. Exrs: Wife, William F. Stribling, Francis McLendon.

Wit: Joseph Gardner, N. G. Barksdale.

Page 367 SNELSON, NATHANIEL. Aug. 10, 1864; Sept. 5, 1865. To Wife Bethany. To my two gr. sons (the sons of deceased son Timothy Snelson) when 21 years of age. Exrs: Sons John R. and Wm. D. Snelson.

Page 316 STROTHER, THADEUS A. Mch. 3, 1862; June 2, 1862. To wife Ella V. Stother. To son Henry J. Strother, minor. Exr: My Father, T. H. Strother. Wit: David Campbell, Thos. A. Strother, Chapley A. Campbell.

Page 34 STROZIER, PETER. May 8, 1837; May 5, 1839. To wife Priscilla. Mentions his Mother Margaret Strozier. Sons, John M. Strozier, Peter J., and Jacob P. Strozier. To daus. Priscilla Strozier, now Woolbright, Mary B. Strozier, now Thrash, son-in-law John Thrash. Exrs: Major I. T. Irvin, brother Reuben Strozier, son Peter Strozier. Wit: Jacob Nash, Jesse Evans, Geo. W. Johnson.

Page 226 SUTTON, MOSES. June 13, 1855; June 31, 1855. To wife all lands, horses, negroes with exception of Daniel Shumate place. To dau. Amelia Sutton. To son John A. Sutton. To son William James Sutton (or Wm. and James). Mentions gr. children by dau. Letitia Kendall. To dau. Sarah Turner. To gr. children by dau. Nancy Talley. To my gr. children by dau. Partheny Williams. To son John A. Sutton. Exrs: Thos. G. Glaze, Wm. D. Quinn. Wit: Wm. L. Anderson, Geo. W. Anderson, John A. Truslow.

Page 185 TERRELL, H ENRY. July 25, 1851; Nov. 1851. To wife. Robert Terrell, my gr. son. My son Joel H. Terrell, gdn. To daus. Ann W. Terrell, Sarah B. Terrell, Mrs. Sabrina Terrell, widow of Thomas Terrell. Exr: Joel H. Terrell. Wit: A. J. Massengale, B. T. Bowdre.

Page 284 TERRELL, SABRINA. Mch. 13, 1855; Nov. 6, 1860. To Thomas Wingfield and James N. Wingfield. Exrs: Niece Susan Wingfield and her dau. Leonora Wingfield. Wit: J. R. Snead, E. M. Burton, F. G. Wingfield.

Page 27 TERRELL, THOMAS. Jan. 1, 1838; Sept. 3, 1838. To wife Sabrina. To brother Henry Terrell a lot in Washington, Wilkes Co. called the Smith lot. To James N. Wingfield a lot for a house, near public square. Exrs. to put a house on the lot. To sister Fanny Branham a lot in Washington bought of Lewis Brown. The lot to James N. and Frances G. Wingfield, in trust for their Mother and for their children. Exrs: Brother Henry Terrell, Samuel Barnett, James N. and Frances G. Wingfield. Wit: Francis G. Wingfield, Obediah Wynn.

Page 161 THOMAS, ELIZABETH. Of Wilkes Co., July 3, 1847; July 7, 1848. My executors to sell all landed estate; the Watkins tract at five thousand dollars; the Mill tract at one thousand; another Mill tract, three thousand; Thurmond tract, two thousand. To nephew James Marks to have all my negroes on condition that he is to pay said negroes three hundred fifty dollars, to each negro, upon receipt of each negro, twenty-one years of age; all other personal effects, carriage and match horses including plantation whereon I live, to be sold. To niece Sarah Hawkins, to children of my niece Susannah Pinkard, cash to each. To niece Martha Williams cash. To each negro one hundred dollars. Balance of estate to nephews and nieces equal shares. Exrs: Nephew James Marks and my old friend Lemuel Wootten. Wit: Three Justices of Inferior Court attested this Will. Codicil: I revoke that part of the Will which says equal distributive shares to William and Luke Williams, my nephews, and my niece Emily C. Smith. I give that part that would come to my nephew William Williams to William Coats his nephew; and the part that would have come to Luke Williams I give to Susan Pinkard's children: That part given Emily E. Smith I give to her Mother Eleanor Crain. July 3, 1848.

Page 104 THOMAS, JOHN. Sept. 18, 1844; Nov. term 1844. To brother George Thomas or his heirs, my entire estate. Exr: Ira Christian of Elberton, Ga. Wit: John L. Wynn, Isaac Briggs, James McMillan.

Page 236 THOMPSON, JOHN D. May 1855; Sept. 15, 1835. To Mr. Manning's wife $2,000. To my niece Lydia Eastwood and her two children, Joseph and Rebecca Eastwood, cash. To Benjamine Roger's wife, dau. of my deceased brother James Thompson, and her son James Rogers. To nephew Bradford Thompson, cash. To Nephew Henry Thompson $5000.00. To E. Brake, cash. To my relative Matthew Eastwood, son of my niece, Lydia Eastwood, cash. All my negroes to be allowed to choose their own masters. Rest of my estate to be divided between Bradford and Henry Thompson, sons of my brother James Thompson. Exr: Frances James Robinson, dec. Wit: John Jesse, Richard F. Gilbert, Samuel Hammock.

Page 22 TRUETT, PURNELL. Nov. 12, 1833; Sept. 3, 1838. To wife Rachael. To Sally Montgomery. To Nancy Collins. To heirs of my son Riley Truett, dec. To my other children: Thomas, Nathan, Purnell and John Truett, or their lawful heirs. Exrs: Sons Thomas and Purnell. Wit: Geo. W. Johnson. I. T. Irvin, Elijah Dearing.

Page 107 TUCK, JOSIAH. Oct. 13, 1843; Sept. 1844. To dau. Susannah McLaughlin. To daus: Sarah Kent, Nancy Colley, Mary Huell, To sons Claborn Tuck, Benj. N. Tuck. To gr. dau. Tabitha C. Huell. Mentions his youngest daus., Tabitha and Martha Tuck. Exrs: Son Benjamine and Luke Turner. Wit: Rachard Barrett, Daniel M. Irvin.

Page 192 TUCK, MARTHA. Sept. 10, 1851; July 6, 1852. To brother Benjamine W. Tuck. To sister Tabitha Tuck. Exr: Bro. Benjamine. Wit: Luke Turner. Luke Turner, Jr.

Page 272 TURNER, LUKE. Mch. 1857; Mch. 27, 1860. To gr. son Luke M. Turner. To son, Wm. G. Turner. Exrs: Son, Luke Turner. Dau. Mary E. J. Favor. Wit: James D. Willis, I. T. Irvin.

Page 329 WALLACE, BENJ. Dec. 23, 1861; Dec. 1, 1862. To wife Frances. Son Marion D. Wallace. To son-in-law, Elishia C. Hickson and wife Celia Ann Hickson. To gr. dau. Ann William Wallace, dau. of Wm. L. Wallace. To Sarah Wallace. To sons John B. and James J. Wallace; the children of Newton W. Wallace, and to the children of Thos. J. Nall, equal shares. I require my executors not to separate the negro families. Exrs: James Wallace, Wm. M. Reese. Wit: Sam Barnett, S. M. Crenshaw.

Page 362 WALLER, NIMROD. Dec. 1, 1864; Dec. 5, 1864. To wife Martha, all estate for life; at her death to be divided into five shares. To Mary Norman's surviving children. To Nancy Goulsby's surviving children. To Getha? Curry's children. To Charlotte Hurley's surviving children. To Henrietta Watkins. To Penina Waller a negro, to go to Elizabeth Eades if Penina is without heirs. Gifts to Georgia Baptist Convention. Exrs: Benjamine Fortson, Benj. B. Waller. Wit: W. D. Quinn, B. J. Quinn.

Page 74 WELLBORN, ABNER. Aug. 16, 1835; Sept. term 1842. To wife Martha. All my children to share equally. To my son Wilkes Wellborn. Exrs: Wife, Nicholas Wiley. Wit: W. J. Carter, Jamison Mabry, W. F. Shorter.

Page 334 WEST, JOHN Q. Feb. 7, 1854; July 16, 1863. To wife Elizabeth O. West, all estate. Mentions Sarah T. Gresham, wife of James D. Gresham. Exr: Son, Thomas B. West, son-in-law, John B. Wilcoxson.

Page 235 WHEATLEY, JOSEPH. Mch. 22, 1852; Sept. 1855. To daus. Sarah, Eastar Rhodes, Elizabeth Collins, Nancy and Sarah Wheatley. To gr. dau. Mary Ann Powers. To gr. children by my dau. Mary McDermot. Exr: Wm. D. Quinn. Wit: Kimbro S. Turner, John M. Booker, Franklin W. Danner.

Page 252 WHEATLEY, NANCY. Oct. 1856; Jan. 26, 1857. To daus. Elizabeth Wheatley, Lucy V. and Martha L. Wheatley. Sons: William J. and Joseph Wheatley, David Hyde and wife Esther. To gr. children of Sarah Wheatley, dec. Exr: John A. Truslow. Wit: Beverly Barksdale, E.W. Anderson.

Page 99 WILKINSON, JOHN. Jan. 1, 1844; May 6, 1844. To wife Henrietta all my estate and riding carriage. Wife to share equally with all my children; to use the estate for support and education of my children.

Exr: Wm. S. Hearn. Wit: Wm. M. Jordan, Ben. W. Fortson.

Page 189 WILLIAMSON, MARY. Dec. 2, 1851; Mch.1852. To dau. Mary Cofer. To sons Joshua C. Williamson, John C. Williamson. To my dau. Roxana Strozier. Exr: Gideon B. Norman. Wit: Winifred and Seaborn Callaway, Sr., John W. Heard, J. I. C.

Page 262 WINGFIELD, ANN N. Sept. 20, 1859; Oct. 28, 1859. To Ann Elizabeth the dau. of Francis G. Wingfield. To sister Sally Pettus, To James A. Nesbit, in trust for my niece Frances R. Nesbit. To children of Montgomery Wingfield, in trust for use of Cornelia Golucke and Leonara Wingfield, until Sally Pettus becomes a widow. Exr: James A. Nesbit. Wit: C. W. Pope, E. J. Pope, Wm. M. Reese.

Page 363 WINGFIELD, GARLAND. Aug. 15, 1864; Feb. 5, 1865. To wife Rebecca certain property for life. To Sarah G. Pettus for her life-time. After death of my wife, to J. S. Lane and wife Elizabeth, all remainder of my estate to James H. Lane and wife; he to pay to Rebecca Wingfield, dau. of Charles Wingfield $1000.00, and to Garland Turner, son of Luke Turner, $1000.00. If any of negroes are dissatisfied exr. to sell to such persons as negroes select. Exr: Wife Rebecca. Wit: Jas. E. Woddy (Waddy), James D. Smith, F. G. Wingfield.

Page 140 WINGFIELD, MARY. May 4, 1843; Mch. 1843. To son Overton Wingfield, all estate. Exr: Garland Wingfield. Wit: John Pettus, A. L. Rakestraw, Simeon Hester.

Page 322 WINGFIELD, SARAH S. Mch. 28, 1862; July 1862. To son Asbury Tate a negro Alford which is one of the Tate negroes. All estate to two daus. Sarah J. Wingfield and Frances S. Wingfield, to be theirs upon marriage. If no heirs, the property to go to Asbury Tate. Exrs: Samuel W. Winn, Wm. Reese.

Page 352 WINGFIELD, SUSAN. Feb. 19, 1859; Apr. 28, 1864. To single dau. Leonora. To children of Francis G. Wingfield. To children of James N. Wingfield. To children of Sarah Ann Reese, my deceased dau. To children of Cornelia S. Golucke. To Thomas T. Wingfield.
Codicil: Nov. 3, 1863. Lenora to have the home place, Exrs: Sons Francis G. and Thomas T. Wingfield. Wit: Wm. Ahern, Chenoth Callaway, Wm. M. Reese.

Page 286 IRVIN, ISAIAH T. Jan. 31, 1860; Nov. 6, 1860. All estate to be divided equally among my wife and children. My children to be well educated. In employment of overseers, I desire my executors to employ such only as are steady, faithful and humane and to be discharged at once if not suitable. Exrs: Sam Barnett, Oliver Battle. Wit: Jas. L. Smith

WILKES COUNTY

ORDINARY'S OFFICE

ABSTRACTS OF ORIGINAL MARRIAGE LICENSES

GROOM	BRIDE	DATE MARRIED
Nathaniel Simons	Nancy Griffin	1793
Leonard Philips	Fanny Brown	1794
Nathan Anderson	Sarah Nelson	1794
Elisha Brewer	Polly Black	Mar. 2 ,1793
William Johnson	Nancy Hill	1793
Henry Wells	Ann Richey	Oct.26, 1793
Herod Roberts	Elizabeth Atkins	1793
John Hardeman	Nancy Collier	1792
Armisted Atkins	Sally Thomas, dau. of John Thomas	1793
Wm. Bryant	Polly Barnett (date illegible)	
Eldred Crews	Susannah Russell	1792
Wm. Binns	Tabitha Freeman	1792
John E. Little	Mary Little	1813
John Lawson	Mary Matthews	1819
Young Johnson	Catherine Willis	1819
James Cunningham	Susan Evans	1820
Joseph Echols	Unity Moore	
Joseph A. Green	Margaret Taliaferro	
James Daniel	Eleanor Ruddle	1819
Stephen Boker ?	Eliza Coalney ?	
A. Montgomery	N. Chafin	1819
Wm. Miller	Sarah Dearing	
Giles Jennings	Mary Stark	
Thomas Freeman	Elizabeth Fouche	
John Thrash	Mary Strozier	
Robert Cade	Orra ? Fullilove	
Joseph Edge	Margaret C. Flint	
Charles Dodson	Ann Knox	
James Hitchock	Betsy Davis (her father Jonathan Davis)	July 27, 1799
Basil W. Bridgeman	Ann Goodwin(License Herred Goodwin, father of Ann)	Feb. 10, 1792
Sanders Stallings	Lucy Bealle	Oct. 22 ,1809
Thomas Hicke	Winnie Bugg, dau. of John Bugg-License	Feb. 27, 1792
Richard Holt	Sally Groce	Aug. 15, 1794
John Hudges	Peggy McKnight	Sep. 29, 1792
David Hurley	Mary Gunn or Mary Green(James Hurley Bondsman)	Jan. 29, 1800
George Hughes	Ann Wootten	Oct. 9, 1811
James Hamner	Patsy Cooper	Sep. 2, 1817
James Hackney	Patsy Ogletree	Oct. 3, 1816

WILKES COUNTY - ORDINARY'S OFFICE

GROOM	BRIDE	DATE MARRIED
Jesse Heard	Elizabeth Right	Feb. 14, 1811
George Hickson	Sarah Evans	Dec. 25, 1817
Josiah H arding	Lucy Stokes	Feb. 19, 1811
Darby Henley	Sarah Slayton (John Henley, Jr. Bondsman)	Aug. 24, 1792
Middleton Harrison	Lucinda Hendley	Dec. 14, 1811
Barnard H eard	Nancy Young	Apr. 26, 1812
William Henderson	Lucy Davis	Jan. 30, 1817
Warner Hubbard	Harriett Harris	Oct. 14, 1813
John Huguley	Susannah Walker	Mar. 11, 1817
John Hopkins	Sally Wolf	Sep. 19, 1816
Seaborn Aycock	Dolly Bailey	Nov. 25, 1813
John Cooper	Rebeccah Holmes Bondsmen Sec. John Cooper Benj. Holmes	Dec. 24, 1793
Elisha Brewer	Polly Black	Mar. 2, 1793
John Walker & Elisha Brewer (Sec)		
Joseph Ford	Anney Pullen	Oct. 4, 1811
John Heard	Annie Boren	Mar. 15, 1812
Thomas Hudspeth	Nancy Hughes	Dec. 19, 1802
Timothy Smith	Polly Taylor	Feb. 5, 1802
Nicholas Sheats, J. P.		
Thomas Wilson	Annie Fry	Jan. 15, 1810
Joseph Roberts	Elizabeth Watts	Sep. 8, 1793
Jno. Watts, Sec.		
Henry Terrell	Nancy Blakey	Sep. 5, 1811
Stephen Williams	Jane Black	Nov. 26, 1810
James Walker	Rebecca Patterson	Apr. 6, 1806
Meshack Turner	Mary Ann Robertson	June 15, 1809
Signed by Jno. Robertson		
Robert Ware	Judith Green	Oct. 20, 1808
Remark: Judith was a widow Robert Ware & family went to Alabama		
John Partrige	Royalinda Coats	Oct. 2, 1811
Garland Wingfield	Sarah Billingsley	Sep. 3, 1812
p. 21, Bk. 1806 to 1824		
John Wright	Barsheba Melear	Sep. 29, 1808
James Callaway	Tabitha Thurmond	Dec. 3, 1834
Thomas L. Cofer	Mary H. Petteet	Sep. 26, 1830
Newton Cooper	Martha J. Slaton	July 31, 1834
Anderson L. Chaffin	Sarah P. Rutledge	Feb. 18, 1834
Edward Chaffee	Asenith Willis	Sep. 11, 1834
George W. Chatfield	Catharine A. Johnson	Mar. 15, 1834
Evan T. Davis	Sarah J. Motes	Mar. 19, 1835
John H. Dyson	Emily C. Sneed	Oct. 10, 1832
Thomas Dodson	Eliza Brandon	Oct. 17, 1834

WILKES COUNTY MARRIAGES
Ordinary's Office

GROOM	BRIDE	DATE MARRIED
Daniel C. Daniel	Elizabeth C. Favor	Nov. 6, 1828
William C. Dent	Catharine Pool	May 15, 1834
John Davis	Harriett Woodruff	Sep. 25,1834
John T. Deering	Emma Frances Stone	Mar. 24, 1836
Clark Echols	Easter Nash	Apr. 10, 1834
Hezekiah L. Embry	Elizabeth Slaton	May 4, 1834
Micajah N. Eley	Ann S. Moore	Dec. 23, 1835
William H. Freeman	Susan Watkins	May 10, 1835
George Florence	Ann McLaughter	Sep. 10, 1834
Roland Formby	Elizabeth Hindsman	Jan. 30, 1834
Benjamine Gresham	Elizabeth Martin	Nov. 13, 1834
Samuel H. Goolsby	Emily Leprester	Jan. 8, 1834

INDEX

Wilkes County, Georgia,

Wills and Marrigaes.

- - - -

ADAMS, F. H. 30; John Quincy 40; Martha 40; Zelotes 40.
AGEE, Emily 50.
AHERN, Wm. 59.
ALEXANDER, Adam 47; A. L. 40, 45.
ALLEN, Reuben 3.
ALLISON, Rebecca 35.
ANDERS, Nancy 11.
ANDERSON, Andrew 35; Daniel M. 40; Edmund 35; E. R. 27; Edward R. 35, 47; E. W. 48, 58; Geo. W. 56; Hulda 4; James 5, 35; James M. 10, 54; James R. 35, 54; Marg't 11; Mary 37; Nathan 60; Richard 4; Sarah Pope 10; Sophia 12; Thos. 13, 17, 35, 55. Wm. D. 55; Wm. L. 48, 56; Wm. Q. 4, 12, 25, 32, 35, 41, 47.
ANDREWS, Anulett 39; Fannie 39; Garnett 29, 35, 39, 52; Garnett, Jr., 39; Henry F. 39; John F. 39; Marshall 39; Metta 39; Wm. 21.
ANTHONY, Ann 35; Anselm 6, 13; Augustus 6; Betsy 13; Bolling 13; Edwin 35; E. Du Bois 35; James 13, 35; Joseph 6, 13; Joseph, Jr. 13; Joseph, Sr. 13; Joseph C. 6, 13; Julia 35; Mark 9, 13; Mary R. 35, 36; Matthew 35; Micajah 6, 13; Micajah T. 36, 55; Nancy 35; Willie 35.
APPLING, Burwell 29, 36; Harman 36; Joel 36; John 36; Lewis 36; Mary 36; Samuel Lewis 36; Thomas 36.
ARMER, Amanda E. 36; Thos. Bolton 36.
ARMOUR, Newton D. 48.
ARMSTRONG, Elizabeth 36; Francis C. 26, 53; James (Rev.) 36.
ARNETT; Ann 7, 11; Marg't 11; Mary 11; Nancy 11; Oliver C. 8; Samuel 11; William 11.
ARNOLD, Allen J. 36; Ann 17; Daniel 49; Chloe Ann 34; Eunice 36; Louisa 46; Moses (H.) 36; Oliver H. P. 36; Richard P. 36; Simon C. 36; Stephen 34; Wesley P. 52.
ASKEW, Isabella 46.
ATKINS, Armisted 60; Elizabeth 60.
AUGHTRY, Catherine 31, 35; David 31; Josephine A. 35, 49; Wm. H. 35, 49.
AUSTIN, Jane 2.
AYCOCK, Presley 50; Seaborn 61.

BABER, Wm. 16.
BACON, Isabella 46.
BAILEY, Betsy 36; Car 36; Delilah 36; Dolly 61; Elizabeth 5; Feby 5, 7; Geo. 5, 7, 36; Geo. Reed 5, 7; Geo. S. 36; Gracey 36; John 7, 36; John H. 36; Josiah 5, 7; J. W. 20; Peggy 5, 36; Peggy Dozier 5; Polly Ann 5, 7; Rose 20; Russell 5, 7, 36; Sarah Ann 36; Simon 36.
BAILY, Amanda 53, Ephraim 53.
BAIRD, Benj. 37; Catherine 37; James 37; John P. 51; Serena R. 37; Sarah Frances 50; Wm. 37; Wm. R. 37.
BAKER, Sarah 36; Stephen 60; Wm. F. 49.
BALL, D. S. 29; Eliza 29; Fred 29.
BANKS, Wm. 14.
BANKSTON Hyrom 37; Lawrence 37; Nancy 37; Weldon L. 37.
BARKER, Wm. 11.

BARKSDALE, Mrs. 35; Beverly 58; James 37; N. G. 56; Susannah 2.
BARKSWELL, Stephen W. 32, Susan 32.
BARNARD, Zadock 5.
BARNES, Henry 6, Lucy Ann 6; Wm. 6.
BARNETT, Augustus 37; Eliza W. 37; Elizabeth 37; Emma M. 37; Mary L. 37; Patrick 5, 33; Patrick J. 48; Polly 60; Samuel 37, 51, 53, 56, 57, 58, 59; Samuel J. 37.
BARRETT, John 24; John P. 33; Lewis 22; Mary 22; Milton R. 28; Nancy 22; Permelia 22; Rachard 57; Robert 22; Sarah 28.
BARRON, David 7; Sallie 7; Sam'l 7.
BARTON, Caroline 13; Clary Fortune 13; Elizabeth Ann Matilda 13; Fanny 13; Dr. Geo. W. 36; Gibson 13; Larkin 13; Lucy 13, 33; Luke 33; Martha Washington 13;
BATES, Anderson 23; Evan 42; Hannah 42; James 23; John 23; John W. 23; Rhoda 23.
BATTLE, Martha S. 46; Oliver 59; O. L. 51.
BEALL, John 6, Joseph 6; Lloyd A. 6; Mary 6; Nathan 6; Polly 6.
BEALLE, Albert A. 33, John A. 33; Joseph 33; Joseph H. 33; Lucy 60; Mary 33; Mary H. 33; Wm. M. 33
BEASLEY, Royland 26, 35, 51.
BELL, John 7, 37; Loyd 9; Mary Lasley 9; Phoebe Bailey 7; Polly Ann 7, 37.
BELLAMY, Caroline 45; Elizabeth 45.
BELT, Dr. L. C. 28.
BENNETT, Frances 46; Peter 46; Wm. 18.
BENSON, America 37; Jane 37; Joseph A. 37; Josephine 37; Lumpkin 37; Martha 37; Pierce 37; Sarah 37; Sarah Eliz. 37; William 37.
BENTLEY, Ann 14; Daniel 13, 14; James 53; John 21, 53; John H. 14; Mildred 14; Milly 13; Rob't H. 14; Rachael 51.
BERRY, William 15.
BIBB, Eliza. 12; James 12; Lucy 12; Martha 12; Polly 12; Sally 12.
BIDDLE, Micajah, 25.
BIGGERS, John 23.
BILLINGSLEA (Y), James 4, Sabrina 4; Sarah 61.
BINNS, Christopher 27, 44; Wm. 60.
BIRD, Ann 8; Braxton 46; Eliz. 10; John C. 43.
BLACK, Edward 6; Jane 61; Lydia 6; Polly 60, 61.
BLACKWELL, Rachael Dunston 49.
BLAIR, James 49; Mary E. 35, 49.
BLAKEY, Benj. (C.) 27, 38; Bolling (A) 37, 38; Catherine 37; Churchill (Jr.) 37, 38; James 37; Joseph T. 38; Judith 35, 38; Mark A. 38; Nancy Ann 27, 61; Reuben 37; Thos. 35, 37, 54; Wm. M. 27.
BOKER , Stephen 60. (BAKER ?)
BOLTON, Chas. L. 36; John W. 28; Polly 27, 28, 50.
Booker, Easter 38; Efford (M) 38; Eliza 48; Eliza Ann 48; Eliz. 38; Gideon 7; Hester 38; Jabez M. 38; James 48; James S. 38; John M. 38, 55, 58; Leroy 38; Martha 38; Mary 38; Nancy 38; Richardson (R.) 9, 38, 45; Simpson 38; Thos. J. 38, 48; Wm. Sr. 38; Wm. F. 7; Wm. M. 7, 38, 39, 50; Wm. R. 48.
BOREN, Alfred S. 46; Annie 6; John 8.
BORON, Elizabeth O. D. 25.
BORUM, Benj. 6, 8; Edmund 6; Eliz. 6; James 6; Marg't (Peggy) 6, 8; Mary 6; Sophronia 46; Thomas 6.
BOSTIC, Mary 48.
Boswell, Eliz. 21; Frances C. 21; Geo. 21; Jane H. 21; Johnson 21; Sarah 21.
BOWDRE, B. T. 56.
BOWEN, John 3; Horatio C. 3; Marcia 41, 44; Wm. 4.
BOWLES, Gideon 6; Hannah Crews 6; Judith 6.
BOXWELL, John 5.
BRADFORD, Barsheba 37; Mary Pope 31; Rich'd 37, 38; Wm. P. 48.

BRADLEY, Amy 37; Ann W. 44; Benj. F. 38; Clary 38; Wm.D. 37, 38.
BRADSHAW, Henry 32; Jesse 32.
BRAKE, E. 57.
BRAMLETT, Ambrose J. 41.
BRANDON, Eliza 61.
Branham, Fanny 56; Francis 38; John T. 39; Mary W. 39; Sarah E. 39.
BREWER, Elisha 60, 61.
BRIDGEMAN, Basil W. 60.
BRIGGS, Isaac 57.
BROOKS, Chris. 38; Martha 48; Mary 48; Samuel 8;.
BROWN, Alex. 41; Ann 2; Bedford 13; Fanny 60; Geo. A. 6; Harriet 41; Henry 2; Lewis 35, 56; Lewis G. 54; Lewis S. 29, 36, 37, 39, 41, 49, 53, 54, 55; Lucy 20; Mary 6; Sampson 32; Sims L. 51; Susan 41; Thomas 2, 20; Wm. 41.
BRUCE, Elizabeth 1.
BRYANT, Elizabeth 46; Wm. 60.
BUCKHANNON, Geo. F. (Dr.) 41, 45, 47.
BUCKNER, Eliz. Mabry 7, Rob't 7.
BUGG, John 60; Winnie 60.
BUNCH, Pounch 6, Sarah 6.
BURDETT(E), Almeda 50; Eliz. 52; Joseph T. 52; Marg't 48; Thos. P. 50, 52.
BURDINE, Chas. 23; Clarke 23; Geo. M. 23; John 23; Marg't 23; Matilda 23; Reuben 23; Richard 23.
BURKS, Benj. $. 33;Benejah S. 433; Chas. 33; Fortune 33; Hudson 33; John 33; John H. 51; Joseph 13, 33; Joseph H. 33; Wm. 33; Wylie P 33.
BURNLEY, Ann 2; Eliz. 2; Hannah 2; Henry 2; Stephen 2; Terrell 2.
BURNS, James 39; Martha E. 39; Sam'l Sr. 41; Sam'l T. 39, 40; Silas 9; Susannah 39; Wm. 39; Wm. A. 41.
BURROUGHS, Acquilla 23; Mary 23; Peggy 23.
BURTON, Edward M. (E. M.) 37, 44, 45, 51, 56.
BUSSEY, C. H. 49, 51.
BUTLER, Cora 39; David 26, 35, 49. Edmond M. 41; Edward 41; Francis 26; Francis A. 26; John M. 33; John W. 32; Mary E. 41.

CADE, Guilford 10; James 12, 39; Nancy 10; Rob't 60; William 48, 49.
CAIN, Eliz. 7, 35; John 14; Newton 7.
CALHOUN, A. B. 34.
CALLAWAY, Aristides 39, 49; Aris. R. 27; A. B. 27; Barham 14; Baentley M. 27; Chandler M. 27; Chenoth 34, 39; Chenowith 36; Drury 14; Eliza R. 24; Eliz. 14; Enoch 26, 27, 44; Geo. M. 24; Harriet M. 24; Isaac 24, 33; Jacob 14; James 30, 61; James H. 24; James L. 30; Jesse 14; Job (Sr) 4, 14; Joel 25; John 30, 40; Joseph (Sr) 14; Joshua 14; Lavinia 14; Lewis B. 24; Luke 14; Mary 14, 24, 33; Mary A. 46; Merrit P. 24; Nancy 25; Parker 14, 51; Dr. R. S. 27; Reuben (H) 27; S. 27; Sanborn 14; Sarah A. L. 27; Seaborn 27, 39, 59; Simon Parker 39; Susannah 14; Tabitha 30; Thos. C. 40; Thos. W. 35; Virginia J. 27: Wm A. 24; Willis R. 12; Winfred 59; Woodson 14, 39.
CAMPBELL, Chapley A. 56; Charter 24; David 42, 50, 56.
CARGILE, John 2; Mary 12, 30.
CARLTON, Henry 14; Isaac 14; Isaac L. 14; Joshua 14; Lucy 14; Mildred C. 8; Rebecca 14; Robt. W. 14; Stephen 14; Thos.14
CAROWTH, Alfred 32 (See Carruth)
CARRINGTON, Timothy 41
CARRUTH, Alfred 32 (Carowth)
CARTER, Amos Madison 40; Chas. 7; Donomia 39; Eliz. Frances 40; Geo. W. 6; Jane 7; Marg't 6, 55; Mary 40, 47;

CARTER - continued.
Matilda Jane 40; Nicholas Drury 39, 40; Reuben 40; Thos. A. 54; W. J. 58.
CARTWRIGHT, Polly 8.
CASEY, Eleanor 14; Hannah 14; John 14; Peggy 14; Roger 14; Sarah 14.
CASSELLS, Rev. Samuel J. Jr.
CATCHINGS, Benj. 7, 8; Frances 4; John 8; Joseph 8; Mildred 8; Seymore 8, 24, 31.
CATO, Christopher 43; Rachael 43.
CAULK, Abigail 14; James Patterson 14, 17; Joseph 14.
CHAFFEE, Edward 61.
CHAFFIN*CHAFIN, Anderson L. 61, N. 60.
CHARLTON, Cordelia 54; Francis 10; Jane M. 10; Mary 54; Mary Pray 10; Phoebe M. 10; Sarah 10.
CHATFIELD, Geo. W. 61.
CHENAULT, John N. 37.
CHENEY*CHENY, F. M. 27; Jno. 18; William O. 27.
CHIVERS, Eliz. 27; 21; Frances E. 21; Henry T. 21; James 25; James A. 40; Joel 21; Joel M. 21; Joel R. 40; Nancy L. 21; Thos. H. 40; Thos. Holley 21, 40.
CHRISTIAN, Ira 57; Thos. 45.
CLARK, Elijah 14; Frances 42; H. M. 51; Jesse 7; Sarah 42; Warren Alex. 42; Wm. 42.
CLAY, Eliz. 12; John 12.
CLEVELAND, A. A. 41, 43; Aaron A. 24, 31, 40; Augustus T. 40; Caroline A. 40; Charlotte 40; Ellen R. 40; Emily 40; Harriet E. 40; John W. 40; Nancy S. 24; Thomas F. 40; Wm. L. 40.
CLORE, Abner 8; Abi 8; Able 8; Abram 8; Anna 8; Asa 8; Geo. 8.
COATS, Drusilla 7; John D. 7; Leslie 7-32; Royalinda 61; Wm. 12, 30, 57.
COALNEY (?), Eliza 60.
COFER, John 40; Joseph 40; Joshua 40; Mary 59; Thos. 40; Thos. L. 61; William H. 40.
COLBERT, John G. 31.
COLBERTSON, John 3; Martha 3; Nancy 3; Polly 3; Thomas 3.
COLEMAN, Emily (A) 25, 34; Geo. W. 25, 34; John 25, 34; John J. 25, 34; John L. 34; Joseph T. 25, 34; Sarah (F) 25, 34; Sarah T. 25; Thos. L. 34; Thompson 34.
COLLEY, Caroline 40; Dempsey (C) 40, 51; Eliza 40; France 4; Frances 40, 51; Francis 40, 51; Francis F. 40; Gabriel 4, 40, 57; Henrietta 40; Henry 40; Henry F. 40, 51; John 40; John O(wen) 40, 51; Louisa 4; Martha 40, 48; Mary 4; Nancy 4, 40, 57; Polly 4; Sarah 40; Sarah Ann 51; Sarah E. 28; Sarah Frances 40; Spain 4, 40; Thos. 40; Zebulan C. 51; Zebulon D. 40.
COLLIER, Nancy 60; Robt. W. 16.
COLLINS, Eli 11; Eliz. 40, 58; Gibson 40; John G. 37, 40; Joseph S. 40; Nancy 11, 57; Purnal 11.
COMBS, Eliz. 33; Enoch 14; James H. 54; Jeremiah R. 33; Nancy 33; Philip (Sr, & Jr.) 14, 32, 33; Philip F. 33.
COOK, Benj. 7; John 7; Joseph 7; Polly 7.
COOPER, Alley 45; John 61; John D. 29, 54; John W. 17; Joseph 45; Lloyd 45; Nancy 45; Newton 47, 61; Newton D. 46, 47; Patsy 60; Rachael 2; Sam'l Jones 46.
CORBET, Eleanor 40.
CORBIN, Mrs. Lucy 11.
COSBY, David 41, 55; Eliz. 41; Lucy 32
COX, Eliz. 41; James 41; Mary Jane 41; Nancy 41; Sarah J. 41; Thos. J. 41; William R. 41.
COZART, G. P. 52.
CRAIN*CRANE, Burton 12, 29; Eleanor 12, 29, 57; Joel E. 12, 29; Warren 12, 29; Wm. H. 12, 29.
CRAWFORD, Nancy 4.
CRENSHAW, S. M. 58; S. R. 47.
CREWS, Benedictine 32, 41, Eldred 60; Emily 32; James 32, 41; James 32, 41; John 41; Nancy 32; Susan 32.

CROSBY, Bai(y)less R. 25, 46; Bailor 32; Louisa 46.
CRUTCHER, Coleman 7; Henry 7; Hugh 7; Robert 7; William 7.
CUNNINGHAM, Anselm 15; James 60.
CURRY, Getha (?) 58.
CUTTING, D. G. 40.

DALLAS, Eliza 45; Eliz. Ann 45.
DANFORTH, Matilda 23; Sam'l 45; Thomas B. 23.
DANIEL, Cunningham 15; Daniel C. 62; Elisha H. 34; Eliza T. 25; James 60; Jane E. 41; Nancy 15; Robt. C. 24, 41; Samuel E. 60.
DANNER, David 41; Eliz. 41; Franklin N. 41; Franklin W. 58; Mary 41; Sarah 41.
DARDEN, Geo. 18; Zachariah H. 23.
DARRACOTT, Eliz. 8; Frances 8; F. W. 51; John 8; Marg't (Peggy) 8; Mary 8; Thomas 8.
DAUBERING, Lapoule 11.
DAVIDSON, Ellinor 15; Hannah 15; Harriett 15; James 15; Jane 15; John 15; Sarah 15; William 15.
DAVIS, A 15; Andrew J. 25, 46; Augustine 15; Batsy 60; Bonita 52; Caroline 32; Caroline M. 25; Catherine 24; Darden 8; Felix 24; Isiah 25; Isiah T. 46; Isobella 25; John 62; Jonathan 60; Keziah 3; Lewis 24; Lewis L. 25, 32; Lucy 61; Molly 15; Nancy 25, 32; Peter 32; Piety 2; Wm. L. 25.
DAWSON, Henry T. 31, 43; Fanny 43; Joseph 19; Robt. 43; Robt. T. 31; Sarah 43.
DEAN, Burket 15; Chas. 15; Geo. 15; John 15; Nathaniel 15.
DEARING, Elijah 41, 44, 57; Emma Frances 55; John B. 41, 44; Joseph M. 42; Nancy M. 44; Sarah 60; William 54.
DEERING, John T. 62.
DELONEY, Martha 6; Wm. 6.
DENT, Michael L. 16; Wm. C. 62.
DICKINSON, Isbel 12; John 12; Robert E. 12.
DICKSON, Martha R. 8.
DILLARD, Sarah Jane 42.
DISMUKES, Nancy E. 31.
DIXON, Geo. B. 8; Marcus T. 8; Martha 8; E. B. 8; Sarah 8; Thos. H. 8; Thos. H., Jr. 8.
DODSON, Ann 44; Catherine 34, 41; Chas. 34, 44, 60; Chloe Ann 34; Geo. W. 34; Harriett 41; Ignatius 34; John 41; John C. 41; Mariah 34; Sam'l 41; Thos. 61; Thos. Ignatius 34; Wm. 15, 44.
DOGGETT, Mariah M. 31; Mary 31; Reuben 31.
DONELLY, Peter 40.
DOSS, Stephen 20.
DOUGLAS, Phoebe M. 10; Thos. 10.
DOVE, Hanson 32.
DOWDY, Henry 17.
DOZIER, Catherine Patman 42; Eliza 42; Eliz. 6, 41, 42; Ezekiel 43; Ezekiel A. 42; James 15, 42; Leonard 15; Martha 42; Rich'd 6, 15; Tilman F. 42, 55.
DRAKE, James V. 27; Sarah A. L. 27; Wm A. 42.
DRAPER, Edwin 8; Lawson 8; Thomas, Jr. 8; Thomas Sr. 8.
DROYHER, Nancy 42.
DUBOSE, James R. 35; Martha P. 45.
DUFFEE, Timothy 38.
DUNNAWAY, Alphena 42; Eliza Ann 42; Henry T. 42; Hiram D. 42; Louisa R. 42; Sam'l 42, 51; William L. 42.
DUNCAN, Ann 2; David 2; Miles 2; Sarah 2; Tabitha M. 45.
DUPREE, Daniel 23.
DYE, Eliz. 42; Nancy 42; Wm. A. 42; Wm. T. 42.
DYER, Thomas 29.
DYSON, John 16, 36, 43, 50; John H. 27, 29, 42, 44, 48, 49, 52, 53, 54, 61; J. M. 36; James W. 54; Wm. 35, 50; Wm. H. 26, 43.

EADES, Elizabeth 58.
EASLEY, Nancy 6; Rhoderick 6.

EASTWOOD, Joseph 57; Lydia 57; Matthew 57; Rebecca 57.
ECHOLS, Alex. 49; Clark 62; Edward 32; Edward F. 39; Joseph 60; Nathan 32; Van A. 32; Van Allen 49.
ECTOR, Dr. Wylie B. 21.
EDGE, Joseph 60;
EDMUND(S), Parmelia 42; Sally Ross 1; Sarah R. 42.
EDWARDS, John 2, 32.
EIDSON, Fanny 7; John 14, 42; Sally 32; Thos. 32; Thos. R. 7, 32.
ELEY, Micajah N. 62.
ELLINGTON, Chas. H. 23; Daniel 23; David 23, 44; Eliz. H. 42; Eliz. M. 15; Francis 23; Henry F. 23, 42; Hezekiah 15; H. F. 43; H. P. 23; Jane 23; John 23; Josiah 23; Josiah Jr. 15; Milly H. 23; Nathan 23; Simeon 15; Simeon C. 42; Thos. J. 42; Tilman 42; Wm. 23; Wm. B. 42.
ELLIOTT, James R. 45; Mariah 45; Thos. 43, 52; Winny 43.
EMBRY, Cinthia D. 29; Eliza J. 29; Emily 29; H. L. 27, 29, 42, 43. Hezekiah L. 62; James 29; John 29; John J. 27; Mrs. S.J. 29.
EVANS, Andrew 46; Arden 23; Arden Sr. & Jr. 42; David 23; Eliz. 23; Jesse 23, 56; Mary 15; Rhoda 23; Sarah 61; Susan 60; Susannah 23; William 23.
EVERETTE, Jesse 8; Rachael 8.

FANNING, Bryan 31; John 31; Malcome 31; Welcome 41.
FARLEY, Sarah 39.
FAVER-FAVOR, Caroline 46; Eliz.C. 62; Howard 30; Isaiah T. 46; James 30; James D. 30; John 24; John B. 24; L. D. 30; Mary E. J. 58; N. H. 30; Mrs. Nancy H. 30; Nancy M. 46; Obadiah 24; Reuben 31; Sarah 25; Susan 36; Thos. 30, 46; Wm. A. 24; W. W. 30; Wm W. 30.
FERRELL, John O. 54.
FICKLIN, F. 47, 55; Dr. Fielding 49; Susannah 7.
FINLEY, David 21; Isobel 21; James 21; James T. 27; Jane 21; John 21, 25, 27; Sam'l 21; Wm 21.
FLEMISTER, Hulda 4; John 4.
FLING, Anna 8; Daniel 8; Jasper 8; John 8; Kitty 8; Thos. 8.
FLINN, Anna 10.
FLINT, Margaret C. 60.
FLORENCE, George 62.
FLUKER, Caroline 44.
FLYNT, Amanda T. 46; Augustus 47; Augustus W. 10, 43; Geo. 47; Geo. W. 10; James H. 10, 27, 47; Mary L. 46; Sarah Amelia 46.
FORD, Joseph 61.
FORMAN, R. L. 30; Rufus L. 39.
FORMBY, John 43; Larkin 31, 43; Nancy 31, 42; Nolan 31; Rich'd 31, 43; Roland 43, 62; Thos. 31.
FORT, Arthur 3.
FORTSON, Benj. 58; B. N. 40; Ben W. 59; Catherine 11; Haley 30; John 48; Marg't 48; Sarah 48; Tavener W. 11.
FOSTER, Eliza 24; Francis 24; John Harden 24.
FOUCHE, Ann 21; Chas. 7; David 42; Eliz. 60; Geo. 21; John 7; Lucy 7; Mary 21; Sarah 7; Sarah Brown 39; Simpson 29; Susannah 21; Thos. 21; Wm. 21.
FRAZER-FRAZIER, Alex. 43, 54; James M. 26; Permelia 26.
FREEMAN, Lucy 9; Tabitha 60; Thos. 60; Wm. H. 52, 62.
FRETWELL, Richard 2.
FRY, Annie 61.
FULLILOVE, Clary 33; Orra (?) 60; Willis 33.
FURLEY, Patrick 21.

GAFFORD, Edny 10; Jeremiah 10.
GARDNER, Joseph 56.
GARRARD, John 43; Martha 43.
GARTRELL, Chas. 10; Joseph M. 9; Lucius 37, 42, 43; Mary 10; Sarah 9.
GEER, James F. 27.

GERMANY, Sarah 2.
GIBSON, John 5; Judah 2; Mary 5; Sylvanus 2; Springer 15; Walter M. 2.
GIDDENS, Edward 32; Eliz. 21, 32; Francis 8, 32; James K. 32; William 8.
GILBERT, Richard F. 57.
GILLESPIE, Edward 51; Joseph M. 51.
GILMER, Peachy R. 19; Thos. 20.
GILMORE, Geo. 20; Hannah 20; Humphrey 20.
GLASS, Thos. G. 56.
GLENN, Samuel 41, 42.
GLENNIE, Mrs. Harriett 45.
GOLUCKE, Cornelia (S.) 59.
GOODRUM, Emeline E . 41; James C. 41; Mary J. 41.
GOODWIN, Ann 60; Herred 60.
GOODYEAR, Fanny B. 18.
GOOLSBY, Samuel H. 62.
GORDON, David 35; Eliz. Snead 7; Lucy 35; Wm. 7.
GOSS, Mary 3.
GOULSBY, Nancy 58.
GRAHAM, Rachael 18
GRANT, Amelia A. 31, 32; Ann R. 21; Augustine L. 21, 24; Eliza J. 24; Ketura 21; Mrs. Mary 31, 32; Thos. 1, 4, 15, 22, 24; Thos W. 21, 24; Wm. 15, 21, 24; Wm. A. 32.
GRAVES, Catherine 43; James 15; James P. 43; John 16; John T. 7; Peggy 15; Robt. C. 15; Sarah 15.
GREEN(E), Chas. R. 24; John B. 26; Joseph A. 19, 60; Judith 61. Marg't B. 19; Mary 60; Thomas 5, 27.
GRESHAM, Benj. 62; Frances 43; George 43; James D. 34, 58; Jane 42, 43; John 42, 43; Kaufman 43; Marg't 43; Martha 43; Martha Ann 43; Nancy R. 42; Nancy S. 43; Rebecca 42; Sarah F.(T?) 34, 58; Susan Paschal 43; Temperance 43; Watson 43; Wm. 42, 43.
GRIER, Robert 4.
GRIFFIN, Ann(e) 3, 15; Drury 15; Eugenia 32; G. W. 20; James 31; John 20; Jno. G. 38; Joseph 15; Nancy 60; Owen 3, 15; Rich'd 3.
GRISON, Rebecca 42. (Gresham ?)
GROCE, Sally 60.
GULLATT, Alex. 46; Geo. 43; Peter 43, 46; Rachael 43; Rebecca 43; William 43.
GUNN, Geo. 22; John 22; Leslie 22; Mary 60.

HACKNEY, Catherine 28; James 47, 60; James T. 49; John O. 25.
HAGARD, Ann 1; Jonathan 1.
HALE, John 12; Polly 12.
HAMILTON, Frances 23; James F. 53; Thomas 10; Wm. D. 53.
HAMMOCK, Hugh 14, John 19; Sam'l 57
HAMMONDS, John 23.
HAMNER, James 60.
HAMPTON, Benj. 2; Thos. 2; Wm. 2.
HANSON, A. C. 46; Catherine E. 30; Eliz. 43, 44; Geo. H. 23; Henry 30; John 44; John M. 30, 44; Marg't A. 30; Marg't S. 30; Mary E . 30; M. S. 30; Sarah 44; W. 30; W. M. 30; Wm. S. 30.
HARDEMANN, John 60; Wm. 2.
HARDIN, Benj. 15; Benj. A. 41; James 15.
HARDING, Harriet 6; John 6; Josiah 61.
HARGREAVES, Christ. 3.
HARKNEY, James T. 41.
HARKRY, Daniel 46; Sam'l Jones 46.
HARMON, Clara Augusta 55; James J. 55.
HARPER, Henry T. 36; James J. 38.
HARRIS, Cornelia Mary 44; Elbert G. 53; Emily 53; Eva Clifford 44; Ezekiel 15; Geo. E. 40; Harriett 61; James 43, 55; James J. 44; Mary 36, 44; Nancy 7; Peter 7; Robert 15; Stephen 31; Wm. D. 52.
HARRISON, Ann 3; Middleton 61; Vincent 22.

HATCHETT, Edward 44; Harriett 44;
HATHCOOK, Sarah Ann 45.
HAWKINS, Eliz. 23; James 12; James M. 30; Sarah 12, 57.
HAY, Chas. 9; Eliza 48; Eliza Lindsey 48; Eliz. 9; Gilbert 9; James 9; James T. 52; Melissa 9; Mildred 9; Thomas 9.
HAYNES, Lucy 46; Sarah A. 47; Sarah Ann 46.
HAYS, Allen 16; James 16; Mary Ann 16.
HEARD, Alex. 24; Ann W. 26; Barnard 8, 16, 61; Benj. 44; Benj. W. 26; Bridget 8; Caroline 44; Caroline W. 26; Chas. 24, 33; Chas. Sr. 16; Charles S. 40; Daniel C. 33; Eliza 44; Eliza J. 26; Eliz. 24, 32; Emily 32; Fanny B. 16; Faulkner 44; Frances 24, 44; Henrietta 26, 44; James 15, 24; James L. 32; Jane Germany 16; Jesse 2, 20, 44, 61; Jesse Faulkner 26; John 8, 24, 32, 33, 61; John Sr. 2, 16; John JR. 16; John A. 29, 32; John G. 16; John W. 59; Judith 44; Marg't 16; Mark 24, 33; Mary Ann 24; Nancy 33; Stephen 2, 8, 44. Stephen Faulkner 26; Thos. 24; Thos. A. 32; Thos. N. 32; Thos. S. 32; Wm. 15; Wm. S. 44; Wm. T. 26.

HEARN, Wm S. 59;.
HEMPHILL, Cyrus T. 24, 31; Emily J. 24, 31; Nancy S. 24; Thomas 24, 31.
HENDERSON, Emma 27; Emma H. 29; Felix 27; Felix G. 33, 44; Felix M. 29; Helen B. 44; Jesse M. 33, 44; Joseph 8, 11, 33, 44; Joseph W. 27, 29; Leving (?) 33; Major 18; Mary 23; Mitchell 44; Peggy 44; Rich'd 44; Sarah M. 29; Simeon 44; Thos. 23; Thos. A. 29; Wm. 61.
HENDLEY, Lucille 61.
HENDON, Sally 9;
HENDRICKS, Catherine 31; John 23.
HENLEY-HENLY, Darby 61; James 49; John Jr. 61.
HENRY, Catherine 30; John P. 30; Nancy 12; Thos. M. 12.
HERRING, Mary 55; Sarah M. 55.
HERRIOTT, Mrs. Eliza.
HESTER, Catherine 43; Sim(e)on 35, 43, 59.
HEWELL, John 32; Joseph 32; Joseph A . 32.
HICKE, Thomas 60.
HICKSON, Celia Ann 58; Elishia C. 58; George 61.
HIGGASON, Benj. 11.
HIGHNOTE, Philip P. 2.
HILL, Abraham T. W. 45; Burwell P. 45; Eliz. 12; Emma 35; Francis 12; Lodowick M. (L. M.) 36, 45; Martha 45; Nancy 60; Sarah Ann Eliza Render 45; Thos. B. 45; Wylie 45; Wylie P. 45.
HILLHOUSE, David 32; David P. 45.
HINDEMAN, Eliz. 62.
HINDSMAN-HINSMAN, Keziah 41, 44;
HINES, Eliza 16; James Sr. & Jr.16; John 16.
HINTON, B. B. 29, 45; Clary Ann 45; Eliza 15; Emma Louisa 45; Fathy Caroline 15; Fielding 23; Fielding Lewis 45; Jacob 26; James 29, 45; James W. 29, 45; Jesse 29, 45; Job R. 26; John 15; Mary 23; Sally 45; Sarah A. 45; Sophia 15.
HITCHCOCK, James 60.
HOBINY, Jesse M. 25;
HODGES, Jesse 5;
HOFF, Ann 22; Chas. 22; Fanny 22; Susannah 22.
HOGAN, Griffin 2; Mary 2.
HOGUE, David 8; Jacob 15.
HOLLIDAY, Allen 25, 45; Allen T. 50; A. F. 25; Franc A. C. 25; Frances Adalaide E. 45; Joseph 50; J. R. 25; Jacintha R. 25; Lavinia Camilla 45; Nancy 45;

HOLLIDAY - continued
Rich'd J. 51; Sarah 9; Syncha R. 45; Thos. 9, 45; Wm. 45.
HOLMES, Benj. 61; Eliz. 2; J.B. 25; Mary 25; Rebecca 61.
HOLT, Rich'd 60.
HOLTON, Hannah 25; Joseph 25.
HOPKINS, Geo. 45; Isaac 45; John 61; John G. 45; Mary 45.
HOPPER, Delilah 42; Jonathan 42.
HORN, Amelia 9; Aspilla 3;John Sr.& Jr. 9; Nancy 9; Polly 9; Preston 9; Sallie 9.
HUDDLESTON, Geo. 5; Susannah 5.
HOUGHTON, John 18; Nancy 18.
HOUSTON, Eliz. 12; Robt. 12; Sam'l 12.
HOWARD, N. N. 45; W. T. 30; Wm T. 30.
HOXEY, Victoria 39.
HUBBARD, Jacob 48; Warner 61.
HUBERT, Benj. 16; Hiram 16; James 16; Moses 16; Viney 16.
HUDGES, John 60.
HUDSPETH, Kitty 8; Mary W. 17; Thos. 61; Warren S. 8; Wm. 17,50.
HUELL, Mary 57; Tabitha C. 57.
HUFF, L. M. 46.
HUGHES, Anith 12; Bernard 15; Geo. 60; Geo. H. 12; Mary 15; Nancy 61; William 15.
HUGULEY, Alley 45; Amos 27, 45; Frances A. 27; Francis 50; Geo. 27, 45; Job. 27; John 23, 27, 41, 44, 45, 46, 61. John T. 45; Lucy 44; Mahala 27; Ransome 27; Rebecca 46; Susannah 27; Thos. 27; Wm. 41, 45, 47; Wm. H. 28, 50; Zachariah 45.
HULING, Andrew 25; Augustus 52; James 31, 52; Sarah 52.
HUNT, Eliza T. 55.
HURLEY, Charlotte 58; David 60; James 60; Sarah 46, 52.
HUTCHINS, Thos. 4.
HYDE, David 58; Esther 58.

* * * * * * * * * * * * * * * * * *

IRVIN-IRWIN, Chas. M. 46; Daniel M. 46, 57; I. T. 42, 56, 57, 58; I. T. Jr. 29, 46; Isabella 37, 46; Isiah T. Sr. 32, 46, 59;
IVY, John M. 53.

JACK, James W. 4.
JACKSON, A. S. 26; David 9; Drury 16; Edmond 16; Eliza Ann 51, 52; Ellender 3; Emmie 41; Franc A. C. 25; Greene 16; Harriet F.10; Hartwell 16; Henry (or Jerry) 3, 32; Jane 26; J. B. 26; Jesse 10; John 3, 16; John F. 46; John H.26; Johnson W. 26; Joseph 50; J. W. 44; Marg't 48; Mary 50; Matthew 46; Mercer 26; Sarah 26, 46; Sarah Horn 9; Thos. 3; Wm. 3, 37, 38; Wm. D. 26; Wyche 16, 25.
JACOBS, Patience L. 53; W. G. 53.
JARRATT-JARRETT-JARROTT, Athali 46; Geo. W. 46; Johnson Terrell 46; Malinda.
JARRELL-JARROLL, John 1; Polly 20.
JEFFERSON, Harriet 51.
JEFFRIES, Harrison 28; Howell 28; Nancy 28; William 28.
JELKS, Ethelred 20.
JENISON, Wm. H. 52.
JENNINGS, Giles 60; Susannah 5; Thomas 48.
JESSE, John 47, 53, 57.
JETER, Barnett 15.
JOCK, Mrs. (widow Sam'l Wellborn)
JOHNS, Eliz. D. 29.
JOHNSON, Alex. 43; Algernon 43; Alphonso 46; Alonzo 46; Catherine A. 61; Chas. M. 46; Cincinatus 46; Geo. 16; Geo. M. 1; Geo. W. 43, 56, 57; Isobel 16; Jacob 46; Jane 40; John 16; John Pope 46; Joseph 22; Lucy 54; Malcom A. 15; Nancy 43; Prudence 16; Rebecca 46; Sarah 9; Sarah C. M. 45; Sarah Murray 9; Stephen 16, 18; Stephen A. 50; Susan 54; Susannah 16; Thos. 2, 16; W. 37; Wm. 2, 10, 60; Wm. G. 41; Young 60.

JOHNSTON, Jacob 24.
JONES, Abraham 1; Adam 3; Adeline 48; Amelia C. 46; Amelia C. 10; Ann 2; Arthur 42; Benj. Welch 47; Dudley 38; Eliz. Crestwell 28; Gilchrist 44; Henry A. 28; James Augustus 47; John B. 47; Joseph T. 47; Lucy W. 38; Martha 47; Mary Frances 47; Mary Louisa 35; Nathaniel 12; Sam'l 46, 47; Sarah 55; Sarah Ann 42; Sarah Harwood 1; Taliaferro 21, 32, 38; Thos. 47; Thos. Welch 47; Toliver 49; Tolliver 40; Wm. 40, 48, 54; Wm. Robertson 47.
JORDAN-JORDEN, Benj. F. 47; Edwin 47; John 47; Joseph 23; Matthew 47; Wm. F. 47; Wm.M. 59; W. N. 50; W. W. 41.
JOSSEY, Henry 23.
JOYNER, John 37.

KAPPLE, Benj. 47; Diana M. 47; Michael 47.
KEELING, A. 4.
KELLY, Barnard 17; Lucretia 18; Samuel 4.
KENAN, Martha H. 12; Owen H. (O.H.) 12, 30.
KENDALL, Allen 16; Allenton 16; Bartholomew 16; Letitia 56; Lunsford 16; Nancy 16; Washington 16.
KENDRICK, Eliz. 38; Greene M. 47; Jacob 44; John B. 24; John R.47; Jones 47; Martin 47; Mary Ann 44; Sarah Ann 24; Susan 44; Tilman (T.) 42, 47.
KENT, Rachael 48; Sarah 57.
KENNON, O. K. 12.
KILGORE, Benajah 47; Chas. A. 47; Mary Ann 48; Mary T. 47, 48; Wm. 47; Wm. G. 48, 51; Wm S.47.
KNOX, Ann 44, 60; Caroline 43, 44; Eliz. 43, 44; Jane 43, 44.

LAMAR, Ezekiel 48; Peter 48.
LANDRUM, John 48; Lettice 48, 49.
LANE, Eliza 35; Eliz. 59; Iverson 52; James H. 29, 35; 41, 46, 59; J. S. 59; Lucinda 35; M. 31; Mark A. 35; Mary 51; Micajah 35; Rich'd 52;
LANGDON, Isaac 23; John 23, 24; Mary 24; Samuel 24.
LASLEY, Catherine 9; David 9; Felix 9; Mary 9; Medium 9; Thos. 9.
LAUGHTER, Henry 17.
LAWRENCE, Susan D. 51.
LAWSON, David 21; John 60.
LAWTON, Alex. R. 45.
LAY, Elisha 15.
LAYSON, James M. 17; John 17; Morgan 17; Oliver 17.
LEE, Daniel 22; Eliz. 49; James 22; John 22; Joseph 22; Nancy 9; Noah 9; Peggy 22; Philip 17; Sallie 9; William 22.
LEONARD, Edward 26; John B. 6, 26, 54; John B. Sr. 7; Ludwell M. (L. M.) 26, 43, 54; Mary 26; Rich'd 34; Sam'l Edward 54; Thos. 26; Thos. Fleming 54; Wm. P. 26.
LEPRESTER, Emily 62.
LESLIE, Mrs. 35.
LEVERETT, Absolom 5; Ann 48; Mary 48; Robt. 5, 7; Sydney 5.
LEWIS, A. L. 47.
LINDSEY, Eliza 48; Isaac 48; James 48; James M. 48; John T. 48; Letitia 48; Sara A. 28; Wm. B. 48; Willis H. 48.
LINICUM, Sarah 3.
LIPMAN, Frances 54.
LIPSCOMB, Booker 32.
LITTLE, Cinthia D. 29; James 1; John E. 60; Mary 60; Sherrod 15;
LOCKETT, James R. 51;
LOVELACE, Sarah Jane 27.
LOW, Daniel 46; John H. 33; Thos.V. 37.
LUMPKIN, John 5.
LUNSFORD, Peter 23; Susannah 23; William 18.
LYLE, David 27; Eliz. 25, 27; James 25; Martha 25; Rebecca 25.

LYNN, Mrs. A. 41.
LYON-LYONS, Edward 33; Eliz. 33; Jacob 33; Nancy 44.
LYSLE, Hugh G. 22; James 21.

McALPINE, Alex. 1; Eliz. Barberry 1; Jenet 1; Mary 1; Robt. 1; Sam'l Major Temple 1; Sarah Temple 1; Solomon 1; Wm. Alex. 1; Wm. David 1.
McBREARY, James D. 29.
McCorkle, Matthew 38.
McCOY, Benj. 17; Jasper 17; John 17; Nathaniel 17; Sarah D. 17; William 17.
McCREARY, James D. 27.
McDERMOT, Mary 58.
McDOWELL, Baptist 17; James 17; John 17; Joseph 17; Marg't 17; Sarah 17, Thomas 17.
McELROY, Peggy 51.
McFLEMING, Jremiah 16; Nancy 16.
McGEHEE, Abner 19; America 38; David 19; Martha 19; Mary 49; William 19.
McGILL, John C. 43.
McJUNKIN, Andrew C. 41; Mary 41; Robt. C. 41; Sam'l 41; Sarah A. 41.
McKEMSY, Cicero 36.
McKENNEY, Augustus48; Cicero 48; Cicero 36; Fanny 48; Geo. 43, 48; Jane 48; John 48; Louisa 48; Marg't 48; Mary 48; Patience 43; Patrick 48; Susan D. 36; William 48.
McKENZIE, John 6.
McKEY, Hannah 15; Littleton 15.
McKNIGHT, Chas. 31, 43; Peggy 60; Susan 43.
McLAUGHLIN, Betty 17; David 17; Geo. 17; Peter 17; Susannah 57; Thomas D. 17.
McLAUGHTER, Ann 62.
McLENDON, Betsy 33; Francis 11, 22, 55; Isaac 55; Judah 11; Martha 22; Mrs. Mary 38; Penelope 22; Simpson 22; Wm. 22, 33.
McLIN, William 17.
McMakin-McMekin, -
McMAKIN-McMEKIN, A. C. 41, 50; Augustine C. 52; Austin C. 52.
McMILLAN, James 57.
McNEILL, John 8; Mildred Catchings 8.
McRAE, James 35; Nancy 31 Nancy A. 48.
McRORY, Amanda 42; Isaac 42.

MABRY, Allen 9, 17; Daniel 17; Eliz. 7; Jamison 17, 58; Jorden 23; Joshua 17; Walton 17.
MAHONEY, Esther Ann 55.
MALONE, Araminta 44; Hazeltine 44; Joseph 44; Joseph 44; Thompson 33.
MANNING, MR. 57.
MARCHALL, Thos. C. 45;
MARKS, Catherine 12; James 29, 57; James B. 30; John H. Sr. 12, 29; Louisa 12; Nicholas M. 12; Sam'l B. 12; Wm. H. 30; Wm. M. 12, 30.
MARLOW, Ann 54; Catherine R. 54; John T. 54; Sarah J. 54; Thos. H. 54; Mrs. Sarah 33.
MARTIN, Austin 4; Ganaway 4; Henry 4; Hugh 12; Isaac 11; John 4, 11; Martha 11; Nancy 23; Peggy 12; William 4.
MASON, Franky 3.
MASSENGALE, A, J. 37, 56; Henry 42.
MATHIS, Griffin 42; James 10; John H. 42; Thos. 10; Wm. 9, 10; Winifred 10.
MATTHEWS, Abraham M. 23; George 3; James 23; John 3; Mary 60; Pricilla 37; Thos. 11; Wm. 31.
MATTOX, Amelia C. 24; Chas. 24; Frances 4; William 4, 24.
MAXWELL, Wm. 29.
MEANS, Gen. John H. 45; Sarah 45.
MELEAR, Barsheba 61; Richard 17.
MERCER, Rev. Jesse 49; Joshua 49; Nancy 49.
METCALF, Margaret 2.

MILLER, Eliz. 18, 35; Israel 18; Nancy 51; William 60.
MINTON, John 17; Mary 51; Wm. 17.
MONCRIEF, Eliz. 17; John 17; Josiah 17; Zilphia 17.
MONROE, Ann 19; David 19.
MONTFORD, Eliz. 9; Harriett 9; James 9; John 9; Theodrick 9.
MONTGOMERY, A. 60; David 11, 31, 49; Lucy T. 53; 31, 49; Nancy (M) 31, 49; Sarah 11, 57.
MOON, Sarah A. T. 54.
MOORE, Agnes 1; Ann S. 62; Eliz. 49; James 4; John H. 49; John R. 15; Mary 15; Robt. 7; Sarah A. T.54; Thos. 15; Unity 60; Wm. 7, 42, 49; Wm. B. 15.
MOORMAN, Amanda 48; Tolison 43; Wm. 48.
MOREMAN, John 52.
MORGAN, Mrs. Ann; 39; Annie 39; Ann S. 39; Caty 3; Joshua 7; Luke J. 39.
MORMAN, James 40.
MOSELY (?), Eliz. 37; Joseph 47; Mary 28.
MOSS, David M. 49; Eliz. v. 49; John 9; John S. 9;Philip 11; Robt. E. 40; Sarah 11.
MOTES, Sarah J. 61.
MURPHEY, Almeda 50; Georgia Ann 49, 50; Jane 49, 50; John 50; John l. 50; Lucy 9, 50; Martha Jane 50; Mary Jane 49; Mary Tom 49, 50; Rebecca 50; Wm. Francis 50.
MURRAY, Sarah 9; Thos. 9.
MUSE, Eliz. 50; Geo. 16; Jackson 50; John 50; Mary 27; Wm. P. 27,50.

NAIL, Julian 2.
NALL, Thos. J. 58.
NASH, Easter 62; Jacob 56.
NEEL, Wm. C. 31; Mary P. 31.
NELMS, Thos. 3.
NELSON, Eleanor 31; Sarah 60.
NESBIT, Frances R. 59; James A. 59; John 15; Sarah 15.
NESH, Acton 18.
NEWMAN, D. A. 26; Garratt 26; Henry J. 26; Nemartha 26; N. 26; Richard 26; Thomas 26.
NEWTON, Mary 2.
NICHOLSON, Benj. 3; Judah 3; Polly 3.
NOLAN, James 27, 28, 50; James W. 27; John 28; John H. 28, 50; John W. 28; Thos. 28, 50; Thos F. 28.
NORMAN, Argyle 50; Amanda E. 36; Eliz. 36, 50; Felix 26; Felix Ann 36; Geo. L. 36; Gideon 44; Gideon B. 59; G. G. 36, 38, 43, 50; Henry W. 26; Irvin 26; Isaac 36; Jesse 58; Jesse M. 50; Jeremiah B. 50; John H. 26, 36; John L. 39; Johnson 26; Mary 58; Mary P. 50; Rachael 36; Thos. B. 39; Wm. 26, 36; Wm. B. 50; Wm S. 50; Willis R. 50.
NORTH, A. 25.
NORVELL, A. G. 23.

OGDEN, Susan 44.
OGLESBY, Garrett 50; Geo. J. 50; Joseph L. 50; Junius S. 50; Martha E. 50; Mary L. 50; Minor T. 50; Shaler H. 50; Temus W. 50; Thos. J. 50; Urbane B. 50.
OGLETREE, Ann 2; John 2; Nancy 46; Patsy 60.
OLIVER, Francis H. 17; Mary 17.
OVERSTREET, Eliz. 11; Wm. 11.
OVERTON, J. Elizabeth 48.
OWEN, Daniel 17, 22, 31; Isabella 17; John 17; Mildred 17; Mary 51; Thomas 17.

PALMER, George 40, 51, 52; Geo. W. 51, 53; Sarah 52; Sarah E. W.51; S. R. 39, 51, 52 (Stephen Robt.)
PARKINSON, Artimesary 51; Eliz. 51; John 51; Levin 51; Rebecca 51; Rhoda 51; Sarah 51; Zadock.

PARTRIGE, John 61.
PASCHAL, Amelia 45; A. J. 49, 51; Dennis 51; Dennis Sr. 51; E. 51; Harris 51; Horace E. 38; John L. 45, 50; Martha Ann 45; Mary Jane 45; Sam'l 43, 51;.
PATTERSON, Abigail 17; Eugenia C. W. 36; Isabella 17; James 17; Jaames W. H. 36; John A. 17; Marg't 17; Mary G. 36; Rebecca 61; Sarah E. 36; Victoria J. C. 36.
PAUL, Benj. 31.
PAVNER, Peter 4.
PAYNE, John 16.
PELOT, John F. 26, 51; Frances F. 26; Francis L. 26, 51; Harriet L. 51; mrs. - - - .
PENROSE, J. E. 47.
PERKINS, Polly 14.
PERRY, Alfred G. 32; Jesse 43; Sallie 32.
PERTEET, John 29; John R. 29; W. R. 29.
PETEET, Eliz. 10, 51; Chenoth 51; John 18; John Sr. 10; John J. 28; John R. 10, 28, 29, 51; John Rich'd 10; Mary H. 61; Mary J. 28, 29; Patsy 51; Rich'd 10; Sarah E. 29; Susan 28; Susan E. 29.
PETERS, Eliz. Hinton 45; Wm. H. 29.
PETRIE, George H. 53.
PETTUS, Caroline 51; Chas. 25; John 39, 49, 51, 59; Mariah 25; Mary 51; Mary Ann 52; Sally 59; Sarah 25; Sarah G. 59; Stephen 40; Stephen G. 37, 52, 53, 55; Stephen R. 39.
PHARR, Ephraim 3.
PHILIPS, Dr. George 12, 13; Isiah 2; Leonard 60; Polly 12;
PHILPOT, Fanny Colbertson 3; Nicodemus C. 3.
PICKIN, John 32.
PINKARD, James (H.) 30; L. N. 29; Thos. 29; Susan(nah) 12, 57.
POMROY, Nancy (E.) 35, 49.
POOL, Catherine 62; David 22; John 52; Mary 52; Stovall 17, 52.
POPE, Alex. 29, 35, 37, 39, 52, 54; A. 39, Ann Anthony 35; Asa W. 39; Augustine B. 23; Barton Chapman 52; Benj. 52; Bolling Anthony 35; C. W. 59; E. J. 59; Geo. 52; Henry 10, 30, 34, 51; John 10, 12, 23; Dr. John 41; John C. 31; John H. 39, 47, 52; James W. 39; Kidda 10; Louisa 39; Martha 23; Mary 23, 31, 52; Rowena 23; Sam'l B. 39; Sarah 10; 39; Sarah Joyner 37; Thos. J. 10; Wm. A. 52; Wm. Henry 52; Wm. L. 39; Wylie 23; Wylie H. 31, 52; Wylie M. 31, 52
PORTER, Abigail 45; Chas. 10; Chas. H. 10; Elisha 45; Frances 10; Geo. W. 10; Fayette, 10; Henry B. 10; James P. H. 10; Martha 10; Nicholas 10, 17; Sarah 10; Solon N. 10; Thomas 10, 17; Thos. C. 10, 17;
POSS, Eliz. 52; Geo. 45; Henry 44; Lucy 50; Sarah 44; Wm. 52.
POUNDS, Garrett 6; Martha 42; Rachael 6.
POWELL, Mary 52; Nelson 24; Sarah Ann 24.
POWER-POWERS, John 42; Lucinda 42; Mary 42; Mary Ann 58; Mary W. 19 Nicholas 19; Wm. 42.
PRATHER, Benajah, 45; Elias J. 52; William 45.
PRAY, Ann 10.
PRICE, Ann Eliza 54; E. 3; Dr. James 54; James H. 54; James W. 54; Susan H. 54.
PROCTOR, B. 27.
PULLEN, Anney 61; James 52; Pleasant 15.

QUARLES, Robt. W. 40.
QUERNS, John 10.
QUIGLEY, B. 53; Chas. 52; Chas. M. 53; William A. 52.

QUINN, Barnet Jeter 40, 58; Sarah 40; Wm. 38; Wm D. 29, 38, 43, 48, 49, 52, 56, 58.

RAGAN, A. B. 21; A. R. 24; Ann R. 21.
RAINES, Henry 18; Ignatius Sr. & Jr. 18.
RAINEY, Mary E. 19; Thos. 19.
RAKESTRAW, Ann 38; Ann S. 53; A. L. 59; Gainham 35, 47; Gainham L. 53; Garland L. 35; G. L. 44.
RANDOLPH, Clifton 53; Dorothy 53; Edmond 53; Henry 10; Isabella 53; Jacinto Dorothy 53; Louisa Maria 53; Mariah J. 10, 53; Mary A. 53; Rich'd 53; Rich'd H. 53; Robt. H. 53; Robt. R. 10, 40, 53.; Thos. 53; Thos P. 53; Thos. R. 10.
RAY, John 53; John A. 53; Mary 53.
REED, William 32.
REESE, Ann 46; Martha A. 46; Sarah 10; Sarah Ann 59; Wm 47, 51, 52, 59; Wm. E. 41; Wm. M. 35, 36, 39, 49, 58, 59.
REEVES, B. B. 25; John D. 4; Matilda 4.
RENDER, Mrs. - - - 35.
REVIERE, Geo. G. 53; Hubert B. 43, 53; James J. 53; John K. 53; Mary Frances 53; Martha Jane 53; Polly 43, 53; Sarah Cornelia 53; Wm. A. 53.
REYNOLDS, Rich'd 11; Thos. 11.
RHODES, Ann 18; Catherine 53; Esther 53, 58; Eustis 18; John W. 52; Joseph 53; Sam'l 53; Thos. N. 27; Wm. 53.
RICE, Nancy 11.
RICHARDS, John 3; Peggy 3.
RICHEY, Ann 60.
RIDDLE, Anderson 10, 31; Archibald 31; Asher 31; Dolly 10; Sarah Y. 11, 31; Thos. 31; Watkins 31.
RIGHT, Eliz. 61. (WRIGHT ?)
RINGO, Mary 10; Nancy 10; Nathaniel 10; Polly 10; Robt. 10; William 10.
RIVERS, Wm 45.
ROAN, James 18; Mary 18; Willis J. 18.
ROBERT, Milton G. 40; Sarah 54; Sarah A. F. 40.

ROBERTS, Ann 37; David 15; E. W. 37; Herod 60; Joseph 61; Milton S. 40; Rebecca 44; Sherrod 15.
ROBERTSON, Ann 26; John 26, 61; J. J. 46; Mariah 26; Mary Ann 61; Sarah 26; Wm. 23; W. E. 31.
ROBINSON, Alex. Webster 53; Caroline 53; Eliz. 6, 49; Frances James 53, 57; James 49; John E. 32; J. J. 53; John Joseph 53; Joseph W. 32, 41, 53; Laura 53; Lewellen 53; Mary L. Wingfield 33; Solomon J. 41; William 6, 22.
ROGERS, Benj. 57; James 57.
RORIE, John 5.
ROSE, Catherine 53; Eliz. 54; Henry 54.
ROSS, Polly 45.
ROUNCEVILLE, Mrs. Gracey 27.
ROUSS, Mary 42.
RUDDLE, Eleanor 60; Lee Ann 54.
RUSSELL, Benj. 35; B. B. 31; Mary E. 31; Susannah 60.
RUTLEDGE, Sarah P. 61; Wm. 26.

SAFFOLD, Amanda 54; Martha 54; Reuben 38, 54.
SAGGUS, John 15.
SALE, Jane 19; Leroy 19; Myra 23; Nancy 19; Richard 23.
SANDEFORD, Harris 54; Susan 54.
SANDERS, J. B. 36; Lucy 50.
SANDIFER, Susan 54.
SANSOME, Dorrel N. 19; Eliz. 19; William Sr. & Jr. 19.
SAPPINGTON, Mrs. - - 27; Caleb 37; Martha 37.
SAXON, Mary 1.
SAYER, Robert 12.
SCHUYLER, Caroline 45; Sarah 45; Thos. Hillhouse 45.

SCOLES, James 4; John 4; Mary 4; Rachael 4; Robert 4.
SCOTT, Irby H. 30; Marg't Burdine 23; Reuben 23.
SEMMES, A. 11; A. G. 52; John R. 37; Thos. 37, 45;
SEAL-SEALE, Alma 40; Alex. 19; Anthony Sr. & Jr. 18, 19; Jarvis 19, 43; John G. 40; Mary 18; Mildred 18; Robt. 18.
SHANK, America 54; Caroline Frances 54; Cordelia 54; Felix 52, 54; Geo. 48; Geo. F. 54; Henry 54; Henry M. 54; Mary 54; Susan 54; Susannah 54.
SHAW, Frances 11; Watson 11.
SHEARMAN, James 31; Jemima 51; John 31; John J. 31; Owen 51; Owen S. 31; Thos. 31, 51.
SHEATS, Nicholas 61.
SHEHAN, Michael S. 10; Virginia 10; Virginia C. 47; Virginia O. 47.
SHELMAN, Bell 39.
SHELTON, Joseph 11.
SHEPHERD, Ann E. 45; A. H. 26, 33; A. Haygood 45; Edward T. 45; S. H. 33; Sarah P. 45; Wm. 45.
SHERRER, Eliz. 35; James 9; John W. 43; Nancy 9; Wm. 9, 37, 43.
SHERROD, Benj. 18; Felix A. 18; Frederick H. 18; Mary A. 18; Samuel 18.
SHIPHERD, Albert H. 26.
SHORT, John 46; Nancy M. 46.
SHORTER, Alfred 37; W. F. 58.
SHRUPTRINE, Daniel 18; Israel 18; Nicholas 18.
SHUMATE, Catherine 54; Daniel 56; Frances 50.
SIGMAN, John 1.
SILVEY, Dolford 42; Eliza 42.
SIMMONS, Asa 11, 18; Caleb 4; Celinda 18; David 4; Henry 11, 18; James Madison 4; Jesse 4; Jesse MM 4; John 11, 18; Miriam 4; Miriam 4; Mitchell Taylor 4; Nancy 18; Polly 18; Rachael 18; Solomon 11, 18; Thos. 15; Wm 11, 18; Willis 11,18.
SIMONS, Abram 21; Nathaniel 60.
SIMPSON, Catherine 26; Chas. N. 25; David 26; Eliz. 26; F. F. 28; Felix G. 25; James B. 25; John 25; John N. 25; Mrs. Lucy 9, 50; Susan 47; Susannah 47; Tabitha J. 47; Thos. P. 25; Wm. 25, 26, 49; Wm. R. 47; Wm. W. 47.
SIZEMORE, Benj. 2;
SKIPWORTH, Chas. 11; Fulver 11.
SLACK, Archibald 21; Benj. 33; Frances 33; Geo. 26; Hannah 25; Jacob 21, 26, 40; Jacob L. 21; Jesse 21, 25, 26; John 21, 23, 25, 48; Joseph 18, 21; Lavinia 40; Mary 48; Thos. 25, 26.
SLATON, Columbus 46; Eliz. 62; Frances 49; Henry 46; Martha J. 61; Mary A. 46; Sam'l 46; Sam'l Jones 46; Sarah A. 61; Wm. 21, 46, 49; Zachariah 46.
SMITH, Adelia E. 39; Amelia 25; Benj. 14, 45; Chas. 8, 10, 15, 18; Ebenezer 54; Eliz. S. 25; E. A. 51; Emily C. 57; Emily E. 12; Fanny 54; Frances 2; Francis 55; Francis E. 54; F. E. 48, 49; Geo. 25; Geo. Blakey 37; Geo. M. 26, 33; Henry B. 25; James 46; James D. 59; James L. 59; James M. 26, 33, 49; Joel T. 25; John 18; John D. 51; Lucy 18, 50; Lucy Christian 50; Marg't 25; Mariah 25; Mary 18; Mary H. 26; N. W. 31; Mrs. Permelia 45; Reuben 44, 54; Robt. S. 39; Sam'l M. 26, 33; Sarah Jane 54; Timothy 61; Wm. B. 38; Wm. H. 33; Wm. R. 38.
SNEAD, Eliz. 7; Emily C. 61; J. R. 37, 56.
SNELSON, Bethany 56; John R. 56; Nathaniel 54, 56; Timothy 56; William D. 56.
SPEAR, John 10, 11.
SPEARMAN, John 22.
SPEARS, Delphia 11; Jefferson 11; Joshua 11; Sarah 11.
SPRATLIN, Henry (E.) 26, 39; James H. 27; Jesse 36; Mary 36; Wm J. 50

SPRINGER, John 18; Lucinda Thornton 18; Susannah 18; Wm. 18.
STALLINGS, Sanders 60.
STANDARD, Ann H. 55; Daniel 55; Daniel H. 9; John T. 55.
STANFORD, Mr. - - 54; Frances Porter 10; Oliver 10.
STANLEY, Mary 11, Chas. 11.
STAPLES, Eliza 42, 55; John 33; Judith 15; Sarah 55; Stephen 15; Thomas 15.
STARK, Emma 45; Martha T. 45; Mary 45, 60; Theodore 45.
STARR, Fenton 17.
STATHAM, Augustine D. 11, 17, 52; Lucy 11.
STATON, Bridget 2; Joseph 2; Mary A. 47; S. H. 47.
STEPHENS, Lucretia 18; Martha J.L. 46; Mary 11.
STEWART, Luch Barnes 6.
STOKES, Armistead (A. T.) 13, 48, 49, 55; Eliz. 55; Isabella 35; John A . 55; John C. 52; Lucy 61; Mary 6, 55; Sarah 55; Wm. 6; Wm A. 55.
STONE, Anderson 55 35; Emma Frances 62; Marg't C. 55; Mary 55; Nancy W. 54; Osborn 35; Thos. 9; Wm. 35, 55; Wm. A. 55.
STOVALL, Benj. 3; Josiah 3.
STRIBLING, Augustus E. 55; Chas. C. 55; Frances A. 55; F. M. 38; Milton O. 55; Sarah 55; Thos. 55; Thos. L. 55; Wm. F. 55.
STROTHER-STROTHERS, Ella V. 56; Henry J. 56; Thaddeus A. 56; Thos. A. 56; Thos. H.(T.H.) 42, 56.
STROUD, John 23; Marg't Burdine 23.
STROZIER, Geo. Edward 48; Jacob P. 56; John 18; John M. 56; Marg't 56; Mary 60; Mary B. 56; Peter Sr. Jr. 18, 56; Peter J. 56; Pricilla 56; Reuben 56; Roxana 59.
STUBBLEFIELD, Wm. 7.
SULLIVAN, James 27.
SUTTONS, Amanda H. C. 38; Amelia 56; Jane 43; James 4; Joel 8; John 50; John A. 56; Lottie 4; Martha J. 48; Moses 4, 37, 50, 56; Nancy 50; Thos. 4; Wm. 4, 48; Wm Jas.56
SWANSON, Joel 18; John 18; Pricilla 18; Rich'd 18; Thos. 18
TAIT, Catherine 11, Lawrence P. 11; Lucy 11; Martha 11; Permelia 11; Thos. J. 11; Zemri W. 11. (See TATE).
TALBOT, Elihu 28; E. J. 28; Geo. 28; Geo. T. 28; G. T. 28; Harriet 28; H. A. 28; James C. 28; Matthew 19, 22, 28; M. H. 28; Sarah 28; Sarah A. 28; S. E. 28; Thos. 28.
TALIAFERRO, Ann 19; Benj. 19; David M. 19; Eliza A. 19; Lewis 19; Lucy G. 19; Marg't 60; Marg't B. 19; Martha 19; Mary E. 19; Mary W. 19; Nicholas M. 52; N.W.47., Sally 19; Sophia 19; Thornton 19; Warren 19; Zach. 19.
TALLEY, Nancy 56.
TANKERSLY, Griffin 51.
TATE, Asbury 49, 59; Enos 34; Enos A. 34; Sarah 34; Zimri H. 34. (See TAIT)
TAYLOR, Amanda M. 41; Joseph 19; Mary Ann 41; Polly 61; Rich'd 19.
TERRELL, Ann W. 56; Booker 27; Chas. 54; David 4; Henry 39, 55, 56, 61; Joel H. 56; John 8; Martha M. 27; Peter B. 32; Robt. 56; Sabrina 56; Sarah B. 56; Thos. 56; William A. 32, 34.
THOMAS, Augustine 2; Benj. 2; Edward 2; Eliz. 12, 29, 30,56; Geo. 57; Hannah 2; John 2, 57, 60; Marg't 2; Mary 2; Philip 2; Sally 60; Wm 16.
THOMPKINS, John 12,30; Nicholas 12, 29.

THOMPSON, Benj. 2; Bradford 57; H. 33; Henry 53, 54; James 57; Jesse 14; John D. 57;
THORNTON, Amanda 9, 50; Amanda M. 9; Anderson 9; James 9; John 9, 24, 31; Martha 9; Rebecca 46; Sarah 4; Sam'l 9; Solomon 4, 9; Thos. T.9; Rev. V. R. 35.
THRASH, David 11; John 56, 60; Mary B. 56.
THURMOND, Absolom 19; Ann E. 54; Benj. 11; Eliz. 11; Frances 54; Fielding 12; James 11, 19; Judah 11; Mary 30; Mary Catherine 30; Micajah 11; Nancy 11, 30; Nancy Pope 30; Philip 11, 12; Polly 11; Sarah 11; Tabitha 10, 61; Thos. 11; Thos. R. 54; Wm. 11, 12, 30.
TINDELL, Betsy 4; Lucinda C. 4.
TINSLEY, James 46.
TODD, Amos W. 26; Eliz. 19; James 19; John 19; Joseph 19; Marg't 19; Nancy 19; Wm. 19.
TOLES, Barsheba 20; Frances 20; Hannah 20; James 20; James Jr 20; Lucy 20; Mary 20; Rebecca 20; Sudduth 20.
TOMPKINS, Jno 30 (See THOMPKINS)
TOMLINSON, Humphrey 24.
TOOMBS, Catherine 34; Gabriel (G.) 22, 34, 35; James H. 34; L. C.34; Robt. 31, 34, 35; 36, 48; Robt. A. 32, 34; Sarah Ann 34.
TRAVIS, Martha 42.
TRIPLETT, Martha 10; Martha P. 53.
TRUETT-TRUITT, Alfred 11; Eliz. 11; Indiana 11; James M. 11; James R. 44; John 11, 37, 57; Lucy Ann 41, 44; Martha 11; Mary B.11; Nancy 11; Nathan 11, 53, 57; Purnal (Purnell) 11, 44, 57; Rachael 57; Riley 57; Riley 11; Sarah 11, 37; Thos. 57.
TRUSLOW, John A. 56, 58.
TUCK, Benj. N. (W) 57; Claborn 57; Josiah 57; Martha 57; Tabitha 57.
TUGGLE, Goe. 16; James 16.
TURNER, Garland 59; Kimbro S. 55, 58; Luke 15, 57, 58, 59; Luke Jr. 58; Luke M. 58; Meshack 61; Sarah 56; Wm. G.58.
TWEEDLEY, Susan 46.

U - - - None

VAUGHN, David 15.
VICKERS, R. H. 35, 39, 52; Robt. H. 39, 51; Sally 39.

WADDY, Jas. E. 39, 59.
WADE, Lucy 12; Reuben 12.
WALKER, Augustus 10; Daniel 30; Edward 33; Frances 39; James 12, 17, 61; James Meriwether 12, 25; John 12, 25; John S. 12, 25; Martha 10, 25; Mary 47; Rich'd G. 12, 25, 61; Robt.12, 25; Sackfield 45; Sam'l 17; Susannah 61; Wm. 10, 12, 17,25; William F. 47.
WALL, B. F. 42; Dorothy 28; T. J. 42.
WALLACE, Ann William 58; Benj.47, 58; Frances 58; James J. 58; John B. 58; Marion D. 58; Newton W. 58; Sarah 58; Wm. L. 58.
WALLER, Benj. B. 58; E.(Edward) 42, 44, 53; Martha 58; Nimrod 50, 58; Penina.
WALTON, Mrs. - - 35; A. G. 16; D. 30; Eliz. 8, 51; Isabella 29; John H. 46; J. S. 29; John S. 29; Mary 54; T. J. 45; W.D. 30; William S. 29, 46.
WARE, James 2; Robt. 61.
WARREN, Eliz. 43.
WATERS, Jane 14; Nancy 44.
WATKINS, Henrietta 58; Benj. 51; Lucinda 51; Nicholas A. 19; Susan 62; Wm. P. 29.
WATTS, Eliz. 61; John 61.
WEBSTER, Mrs. - -35; Eliz. ;4 Lucretia 42; Marten 42.

WEEMS, Lock, 41, 42, 44, 45.
Walter H. 44.
WELLBORN, Abner, 34, 58; Abner R. 34; Ann 34; Hepsibah 34; John W. 24; Katherine C. 24; Martha 34, 58; Sam'l 24; Mrs. Sam'l 24; Wilkes R. 34, 58.
WELLMAKER, Delia 54; Elias 54; Eliz. 54; Felix 54; Israel 54.
WEST, Ann C. 31; Chas. Pinkney 24, 31; Eliz. O. 58; John 27, 28, 31, 50; John M. 24, 31; John Q. 25, 34, 42, 47, 48, 58; Mary Ann 24, 31; Mary S. 31; Nancy 27, 50; Nancy Crooks 24, 31; Thos. B. 58; Wm. 31.
WELLS, Hetty 20; Henry 60; James 20.
WHATLEY, Daniel 3; Elisha 3; Frances 3; Hiram 3; Jesse 3; John 3; Michael 3; Richard 3; Thomas 3.
WHEATLEY, Eliz. 58; Joseph 58; Lucy V. 58; Martha L. 58; Nancy 58; Sarah 58; Wm J. 588
WHITAKER-WHITTAKER, Abraham 31, 43; Harden P. 26; Isaac 26, 37; James M. 26; Jincy 43; Sarah Ann 43.
WHITE, James 49; Joseph 31; Sarah 49; Susan 31.
WHITLOCK, John 20.
WILCOXON, John B. 40, 58;
Wiley - See WYLIE
WILKERSON, Samuel 4.
WILKES, R. H. 54.
WILKINSON, Ann 1; Ann Douglas 1; Ann T. 29; Bailey 3, 22; Caroline 1; E. A. 29; Floride V. 29; Frances 4; Francis 3, 4; Hazlewood 1, 3; Henrietta 58; Hulda 1; Jemima 22; Jesse 3; Joanna 1; Joel Jabez 22; John 1, 3, 22, 26, 29, 58; John Jr. 22; Julia 4; Lavinia 22; Micajah 1; Nathaniel 3; Pleasant 3, 22; Pleasant L. 22; Polly 3; Reuben 1; Sam'l 3; Sherard (Sherwood ?) 3.
WILLIAMS, Eliz. 16, 55; Elias 32; Mrs. Emma 27; Geo. W. 38; Geo. M. 27; Harrison 32; Jesse 16, 27; Jesse C. 27; Joseph M. 27; Luke 57; Mark 12; Martha 30, 57; Partheny 56; Peter Taton 16; Sarah J. 27; Simpson H. 32; Stephen 6, 61; Thos. 32; Wm. 57.
WILLIAMSON, Chas. 14; Eliza 20; Jefferson 20; John C. 59; Marg't 10; Mary 59; Micajah 20; Polly 20; Sally 10; Wm 20.
WILLIS, Mrs. - 35; Asa H. 39; Asenith 61; Benj. F. 10; Caroline E. 39; Catherine 60; Eliz. 22; Eliz. E. 26; Frances-Francis 22, 37; Geo. 12; James 22; 39; James D. 35, 58; L. H. 32; Martha 10; Mary Ann 41; Mary P. 31; Nancy 32; R. J. 25, 32; Robt. J. 12, 51; Rich'd W. 12; S. W. 32; Taliaferro 52; Wm 39; Wm. B. 31; Wm. Thos 39.
WILSON, John 15; Thos. 61.
WINGFIELD, Ann Eliz. 59; Ann N. 59; A. J. 53; Archibald S. 33, 34, 37; A. S. 39, 41, 42, 44, 49, 51, 55; Chas.(T.) 33, 42, 59; Eliz. 33; Francis 33; F. C. 53; Francis G. (F. G.) 56, 59; Frances S. 59; F.S. 40; Garland (G.) 25, 47, 59, 61; James 37; James N. 43, 56, 59; Leonora 56, 59; Mary 8, 26, 59; Mary L. 33; Mary Octavia 55; Montgomery 59; Overton 59; Rebecca 59; Sam'l 33; Sarah 34, 49; Sarah Ann 37; Sarah J. 59; Sarah S. 59; Susan 56, 59; Thos. 32, 56; Thos. T. 59; William C. 33.
WINN, see WYNN
WISE, Eliz. 48; John 31; Patsy 31.
WOLF, Geo. 61 47; Sally 61.
WOOD, Drury 54; Polly 54.
WOODALL, Eliz. 20; James 20;

WOODALL, Eliz. 20; James 20; John 20; Jonathan 20; Williamson 15.
WOODRUFF, Clifford 4; Harriett 62; Rich'd 4; Wyatt 4.
WOODS, Bailey M. 12; Citizen S. 12; Geo. 12; Hugh 12; John 12; Josiah 12; Josiah W. 12; Middleton (G.) 12, 13; Peter 12; Reuben 13; Robt Sr & Jr. 12, 13; Robt. T. 12; Saml 12; Wm. 12, 13; Wm. H. C. 13.
WOOLBRIGHT, Daniel 37; Pricilla 56.
WOOTTEN, Ann 60; Caroline 29; C. H. 29; C. T. 29; Eliz. 20; Francis 23; Geo. 20; Gilbert Hay 23; Henry P. 29, 45, 48, 50; H. P. 29, 41; H. W. 29; James 23; Joel 23; J. F. 29; John L. 42, 47; John T. 31, 45; Lemuel 23, 57; Louisa 23; Lucretia 12; Mary 23; Mary E. 29; Mary P. 29; Myra 23; Penelope J. 37; Rich'd B. 12; Sarah A. 29; Tabitha 23; Thos. 10, 12, 23, 37; 50, 52, 55; Thos H. 38; Thos. W. 29; T. L. 29; Wm. L. 29, 45.
WORRELL, Wm. 32.
WORTHAM, Lemuel 20; Thos. Sr. & Jr. 20; Wm 20; Wm C. 20.
WRIGHT, Eliz. 61; Elvira T. 47; James 27; John 15, 46, 61; John M. 27; Wm C. 27.
WYLIE, Adam 20; Eliz. 20; James 20; Jane 20; John 20; Martha 20; Nicholas 35, 36, 58; William 20.
WYNN, Jane 49; John L. 50, 57; Kittie 45; Lemuel B. 45; Obediah 56; Sam'l B. 41; Sam'l L. 49; Sam'l W. 29, 59.

X - - -None

Young, Geo. Sr. & Jr. 5, 20; James 5; John 5; Leonard 5, 20; Nancy 61; Patty 19;

Z - - None

LaVergne, TN USA
15 March 2011
220265LV00003B/4/P

9 780806 307350